To the
Eel Island
An Evening Journey

Charles Moseley

MERLIN UNWIN BOOKS

ELY

A	Egremans ſtret
B	Newname
C	Cats Lane
D	Dounham
E	Cowe Lane
F	Cauſey Lane
G	Tiſle Lane
H	S. Maryes Stret
I	S. Maryes Church
K	High Rowe ſtret
L	The market
M	Brodhiue ſtret
N	Brodhiue
O	Trinitie church
P	S. Peters miniſter
Q	Walkers lane
R	The Gallarye
S	Mount hill
T	Flaxe lane
V	The drawe bridge
W	The Fenns

50   100   150   20

A Scale of Paſes

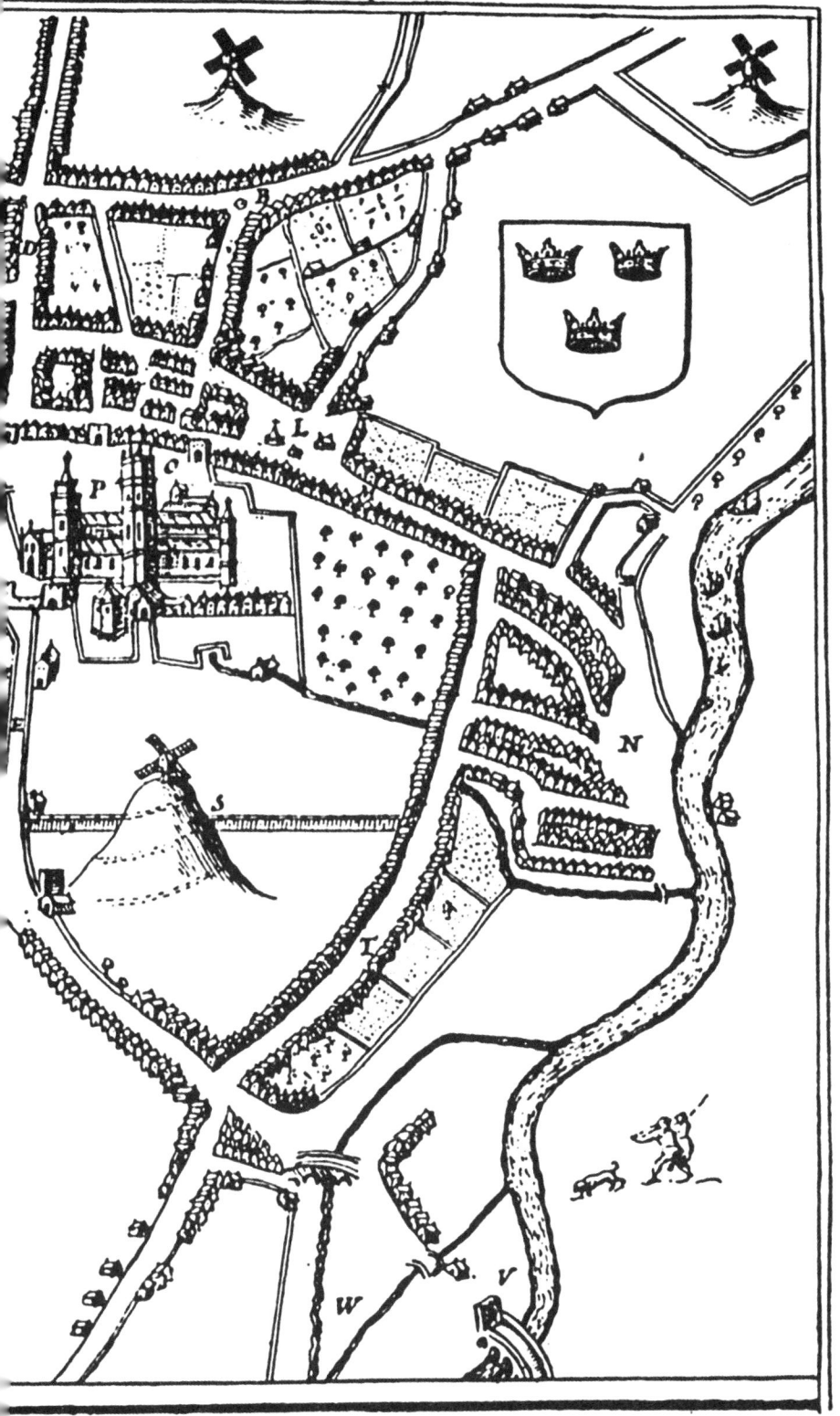

Merlin Unwin Books
6 Rural Enterprise Centre
Eco Park Road
Ludlow
SY8 1FF
UK

www.merlinunwin.co.uk

ISBN 978 1 913159 83 2
Typeset in 12 point Adobe Caslon by Joanne Dovey, Merlin Unwin Books
Printed by Bell & Bain Ltd, UK

Sweet to ride forth at evening from the wells
When shadows pass gigantic on the sand,
And softly through the silence beat the bells
Along the Golden Road...

James Elroy Flecker, *Hassan* (1922)

Thanks

It is entirely proper that I begin this book by thanking the many people who put up with me in writing mode, for all their help, witting and unwitting, in making it. The encouragement of Merlin and Karen Unwin, my lovely publishers, and of the staff at Toppings' Bookshop, from the graceful sash windows of which you can see the Cathedral in Ely, has been immensely valued. There are people I have met and talked to in the street or in the fields whose names I never knew: but they are not forgotten. But chiefest among my many benefactors is beloved Rosanna, my wife, who met me years after the dear wife of my youth, Jenny, had died. It was after her own marriage had ended, when we were both wandering unhappily among the shades.

> ...salimmo sù, el primo e io secondo,
>   tanto ch'i' vidi de le cose belle
>   che porta 'l ciel, per un pertugio tondo.
> E quindi uscimmo a riveder le stelle.

Patience is not my long suit: Rosanna makes up for that. And she makes grand coffee and sandwiches, 'stays me with flagons and comforts me with apples'. It is to the House in Cow Lane, Ely, she found to which we shall fly from this beloved house at Reach: when time is ripe, and then fold our wings.

CWRDM
Reach and Ely, 2025

CONTENTS

Of all the Marshland Isles, I Ely am the queen:
For winter, eachwhere sad, in me looks fresh and green.
The horse, or other beast, o'erweighed with his own mass,
Lies wallowing in my fens, hid over head in grass:
And in the place where grows rank fodder for my neat [cattle],
The turf which bears the hay is wondrous needful peat:
My full and batning [fruitful] needs not the plowman's pains;
The rills which run in me are like the branched veins
In human bodies seen; those ditches cut by hand
From the surrounding meres to win the measured land.
To those choice waters I most fitly may compare,
Wherewith nice women use to blanch their beauties rare.
Hath there a man been born in me that never knew
Of Watersey the Leàme, or the other called the New?
The Frithdike near'st my midst; and of another sort,
Who ever fished or fowled that cannot make report
Of sundry meres at hand, upon my western way,
As Ramsey Mere, and Ug, with the great Whittelsey?
Of the aboundant store of fish and fowl there bred.
Which whilst of Europe's isles Great Britain is the head,
No meres shall truly tell, in them, than at one draught,
More store of either kinds hath with the net been caught:
Which though some petty isles do challenge them to be
Their own, yet must those isles likewise acknowledge me
Their sovereign. Nor yet let that islet Ramsey shame,
Although to Ramsey Mere she only gives the name;
Nor Huntingdon, to me though she extend her grounds,
Twit me that I at all usurp upon her bounds.
Those meres may well be proud that I will take them in,
Which otherwise perhaps forgotten might have been,
Besides my towered fane, and my rich citied seat,
With villages and dorps, to make me most compleat.

Michael Drayton, *PolyOlbion*, 1612

Stirring my Stumps

You know how it is: you have an interesting journey to do, you do not know quite where it will take you, and it is a lovely morning. There is no excuse at all for not getting up and putting your boots on. But somehow... Starting a book is like that. It ferments, so to speak, in your mind, and every so often perfectly formed bubbles rise to the top, and if you don't catch them they blow away on the wind. So you have a mass of jottings, some polished like those stones you find on a beach that fit the hand perfectly, and others of which you can't make sense later when the mental – shall we say flatulence? – has passed. The bigger the pile, the more I keep on putting off the time when I have to take the plunge and get started, trying to put some order into those jottings, trying to convey (and knowing I shall fail, for language never can be the thing it describes) what the experience was that I am trying to map.

So, here we are, at the desk, coffee by my right hand, dog at my feet – but now comes, for me, the really hard bit: the first sentence. I have written much in my long life, and I can recall many a day when I sat at my desk with my pile of notes, from eight in the morning till the long afternoon had passed and the shadows lengthened, and that first sentence simply would not come. Many a time have I given up, and friends were round for drinks or something, and then the sentence would come, inconveniently, for I just had to go away and write it down or it would be lost. All writers need indulgent friends and, ideally, a wife who makes excuses for you – and then, like Rosanna, can put up with being a (albeit sometimes restive) writing widow.

This book is started, at last. You and I, Gentle Reader (I love using that old-fashioned address!) will spend some time together, and before we get stuck in you need some background. Briefly, my first wife Jenny (now long dead) and I, very young and only a year married, bought the cheapest house the estate agent had on his books, in a village we had never heard of. When we told people where it was they said, 'Why?' The village was indeed then very down at heel, grubby, and some people said it was 'a dying village' – it had then some 150 inhabitants, as against 500 in 1900.

But over the 47 years after embarking on that crazy adventure, we came to love both house and village, and when she died suddenly a decade and a half ago, there was little point in moving from the garden we had made, where our children had grown to adulthood, where memories coloured the sunlight through the apple trees we planted. The village has now grown to be most desirable, a place where no young couple could buy as we did.

After a good number of years, by chance – but what is chance? – Rosanna (the real, quiet, heroine of this story) and I met. How matters not: what does is that we did. She has told her own story in her own book – and I do recommend it.* She too had her own house; like me she had two children who had grown up and flown the nest, and she was already planning to return from Northamptonshire to the Cambridge she had loved as a young woman. 'You'll get more for your money in Ely,' said everyone, and so it was.

She liked Ely already, and had good memories of it: her father and mother had regularly visited her when she was an undergraduate at Cambridge and taken her out to Sunday lunch in a restaurant that still exists near the Cathedral. (Moreover, it still offers the same excellent menu.) She found a house that needed the loving care that we could cooperate in giving it, with both of us agreeing that the time was not far off when stiffness in the joints and other ills the flesh is heir to would make moving from the village of Reach to a town – and I myself had never lived in one – the wise course. So the slow move began: building work, getting rid of this and that – very hard! – and a still continuing happy double life of country town and country village.

---

* *Songs from the Suitcase: Inhabiting an Inheritance* (Ormskirk: Beaten Track Books, 2024)

So as I write this book, we are in no hurry, and will happily divide our time between Rosanna's house and mine until the lawnmower becomes a burden and the city calls as the nights draw in. Our such different pasts converge in that Ely house we have made together. But, as they used to say in the Preston I knew as a youth, 'Tha can take a lad out o' t'ginnel, but tha canna take t' ginnel out o' t' lad.' We are what our pasts have made us, and this new present is much coloured by the baggage we carry with us into it. So this book is like Janus, the Roman god of beginnings, looking two ways at once, backward and forward.

Many people as they get older have to face leaving somewhere they have loved, a place soaked in long memories of family and youth, and all the other things, for somewhere more – as they say – 'manageable'. It is different for everyone, and not always easy, for our ghosts go with us, and it cannot help but be emotional. Everything connects with everything else. That is one reason why I cannot resist footnotes: nothing is simple or two-dimensional except maths, and not even then, really. Sometimes the notes get a bit out of hand, like those times on a walk when you swerve off to look at something you have just noticed, or the dog suddenly stops dead to investigate a particularly interesting tree or lamp post. (So, in kindness to all, the longer, numbered, ones are at the back of this book, in the section called Diversions and Distractions). There is no such thing as a new beginning.

This book records just that experience, both of having all those years behind and far fewer in front, and of having to learn that new place to which Time is bringing you – and populate it with its own stock of private memories. Such a move need not be a matter for repining and regret, but a new adventure. We have been blessed in that our move can be slow, measured, no sudden bustle of removal men and vans but a quiet, gradual, confluence of her life and mine, like the confluence of the slow Cam and Ouse a few miles from here on their way to the sea past Ely, only a dozen miles from the house and garden where my children grew up. From that garden, the midsummer sun on its most northerly reach sets over where her Ely house extends its welcome.

We ought to welcome change: it is in the very weave of existence. Indeed, it is what makes our very bodies work. Serendipitously, when we were last in Rome, just a few weeks ago, we had that brought home to us. Going up the steep lane to the top of the Aventine hill, we came to a modern garage. Outside its closed up-and-over door, a new motorbike was parked. On the wall a security camera stared blankly with its glassy eye: a sign of the times. But the lintel was a large slab of marble, on which was carved, in weathered but still beautiful letters that had impassively seen the comings and goings of Caesars and Goths, Popes and Blackshirts, *Omnium Rerum Vicissitudo Est* – 'There is change in all things.' The camera kept its eye on us, just as the informers, *delatores*, in the tyrannous years had watched their fellow citizens.

And once we do come to the final change, having actually stopped, folded our wings – well, who knows? That may be the greatest adventure of all. Tennyson makes Ulysses put it better than I ever could. (He would, wouldn't he?):

We are not now that strength which in old days
Moved earth and heaven; that which we are, we are;
One equal temper of heroic hearts,
Made weak by time and fate, but strong in will,
To strive, to seek, to find, and not to yield.

Tennyson, *Ulysses*, (1833)

Transit and Moonrise

Late summer. The combines have pretty well finished their grazing across the flat fields of the fen. Already a few of the stubbles have had a cultivator through them, leaving untidy brown bits of this last year sticking up where next year will show – one hopes, but nothing is ever certain – new green shoots grasping at the sunlight. Evening. The low sun is stretching out the trees and the marching pylons in long shadows across the golden stubbles. It is setting noticeably further south each day now. I walk across the stubble field on which years ago I used to gather mushrooms at this time of the turning year. I keep the sun behind me, as I used to, so that its low angle could highlight the tiny swellings of the ground which show where the secret bounty is hiding. My shadow reaches a good seventy yards to where Milo the Labrador is sitting, bored with waiting for me to come back to him. He would not like mushrooming, any more than black Hector or yellow Gunnar did before him. In the distance, eight or so miles away by crow and near double that by road or water, I can see the Tower and Octagon of Ely Cathedral, bright as they catch the last of the sun.

All those decades ago, when I first came down from my native Lancashire coast to the soft south, first to study at Cambridge, then to the little village on the Fen edge about which I have written much, I little imagined the place that Ely might come to play in my life.

It was sixty-one years ago when I first saw the erstwhile Island. It was a bright day of early summer, one of those delectable days when it feels like the morning of the world. Indeed, it was, for me. Old as I am, I can remember as if it were yesterday that feeling of elation, physical and mental, sharp as a pin. University exams were over, the pressure was off. (Only later, as I became a don myself, did I realise that those who had been teaching us could not enjoy that holiday feeling, for they were deep in marking what we had deplorably written.) The June sun shone in the most beautiful town I had up to then ever seen. The Chaplain of my College was a man whose enthusiasms were overmastering if not always lasting, whose talents were manifold and generosity infinite. We were not, all of us, quite sure about his sudden passion for the fiddle – unignorable as his playing sounded from his open window across the summer river – but his musical taste was impeccable and he played to the end of his long life. The next passion was antique ivory chessmen, which he collected for a spell, with verve and remarkable taste.

I, who had never before seen anything but crude wooden or plastic chessmen, remember having him put into my hand the delicate red-dyed ivory of a pawn carved into a miniature Portuguese soldier from a set that originated in Japan in the early nineteenth century. The opposing white pawn was a tiny samurai. His questing mind led him to write two good novels when he was in his 80s.

He loved to share his latest crazes with his friends, willing or not. That summer term, his newest passion was a green beetlebacked Alvis of noble vintage, and he proposed three of us go with him to tea in King's Lynn. He could show off its paces – and you do need to have people with you to appreciate that – on the A10. (The A10 then was a quiet road: you might wait a few minutes for a car to come along, and its flatness was a delight under cycle wheels.) I sat in the dickey seat, the wind of our passing in my hair and the throaty roar of the engine in my ears, making conversation, already unnecessary, impossible. The Alvis was indeed a glamorous beast, and we turned many heads as we roared through the villages. And then, from the flatness of the fen past Waterbeach we saw – I for the first and ignorant time – across level fields where long-stalked barley was blanching towards harvest, the low rise of the Isle of Ely. I know now it sits on a greensand ridge with the clay that lies below the fen on the one side and the limey stuff on the other. We came to Stretham – I knew enough to know the name remembered a Roman road – and passed its fine church with the unusual spire, and came to the top of the hill where the mill caught the wind. As we breasted it, suddenly, there before us was the Cathedral's bulk seeming to sail above the Fen, dominating the city on a hill the light of which cannot be hid. It was a moment almost of epiphany: this matters; this is important: but I did not know why.

But an Alvis when wound up brooks no dawdling, and there was then little traffic on the A10. We swung into the town, glimpsed the Cathedral's lopsided west front, then again, as we went round the sharp corner by the Lamb Hotel with a crash of double de-clutched gears, sidelong we looked straight at where the north tower had been before it fell. Then out again into the countryside, through villages and little towns with names as sweet as a nut, Southery, Hilgay, Stow Bardolph, Downham Market, Narborough, every one of them, as I was just beginning to realise, a story.

It was a good tea – triangular cucumber sandwiches on brown bread – unusual then! – with the crust cut off, and many cakes – in an hotel just off the Friday Market, with potted palms in the sun lounge. We saw the Ouse by the Hanseatic warehouse, and smelt the nearby sea. (Did I know what the Hansa was then? I doubt it.) The sea smell recalled with sudden sharpness the smell of the low tide saltings I had known at home. And we drove back in the summer light with the sun westering, and the breeze of our passing was full of the many evening insects of those days. A good day. Dear Michael, on him be peace.

This was my first experience of the true Fens. My childhood and youth had been on a windy coast in sight of the Lakeland hills and the outliers of the Pennines, like Parlick and Snape Fell, which I could see from my garret bedroom window. And now I was for the first time seeing the black-soiled fields of the drained peat fen, which in time would become so familiar. Corn and beet and potatoes in fields rich as I had never seen, fields with ditches rather than wind-sculpted hedges, stretched level to the horizon.

Years and much reading later, I came across how the road of that exhilarating afternoon was seen by a man who enjoyed a late eighteenth century reputation as a theorist of 'the picturesque'[1]. William Gilpin had a considerable effect on how landscape was perceived by those with enough leisure, an aspiration to refined taste, and no need to get soil under their fingernails. Gilpin was not impressed by the Cambridge to Ely road[2], the new turnpike (first started in 1763) for the coaches. (A stone marking its terminus is beside the road just as you enter Ely from the south, half hidden by enthusiastic plants.)

From Cambridge the road to Ely led us immediately among fens. Trees, groves, extensive distances, and all the variety of landscape, are now totally gone. All is blank. The eye meets nothing but dreary causeways;— qua Pontinas via dividit uva paludes. *Stretches of flat, swampy ground; and long ditches running in Strait lines; and intersected, at right angles, in various parts, by other ditches, make the whole of the scenery on each side. In the room of such beautiful objects as often adorn landscape, the only ornaments of this dreary Surface are windmills, those types of exposure; and these we observed, in Some places, accessible only by boats. Their use is to pump off the waters into the channel of the river: in dry summers this is in part effected naturally. But in so flat a surface the water commonly lies long; and in many parts stretches as far as the eye can reach; the road running through it, like a lengthened mole, in perspective.*

Near a century after Gilpin, Charles Kingsley – some remember him for *The Water Babies*, some for his dispute with Cardinal Newman, and some for his youthful prowess as an angler – recalled in an eloquent lecture to the Mechanics' Institute in Cambridge in 1867 what the fens had been only a short while before, when wholesale draining had still to have its full effect. He had watched the destruction of a great natural phenomenon, which had turned 'a waste howling wilderness' (the Great Fen was such in his boyhood), into what he called a 'Garden of the Lord.' Like most of his generation, he recognised the benefits of railways and steam engines powering the drainage far more reliably than the intermittent windmills. (One steam pump, the Old Engine, still survives at Stretham, and qualifies for its own brown roadside sign as Something You Ought To See.) He could acknowledge that the drained fen, which we take for granted, had brought many benefits, and fed the new sprawling towns of industrial England. But he could not help but write lyrically, regretfully, of the loss of the wetland habitats, the richness of birds and insects that they had held: '...dark green alders, and pale green reeds, stretched for miles round the broad lagoon, where the coot clanked, and the bittern boomed, and the sedgebird, not content with its own sweet song, mocked the notes of all the birds around; while high overhead hung motionless, hawk beyond hawk, buzzard beyond buzzard, kite beyond kite, as far as eye could see.'

God knows, it is even more impoverished now, with decades of the pesticides and fertilisers of industrial farming. (But way back in the 1960s, when I first saw the Fens, we had not woken up to the dangers of those miraculous new chemicals.) And I can feel the same sort of regret as Kingsley when I think of what is no more of the wind-combed hedges and little woods that mapped for my youth the sweet, green, lush country of the Fylde in the windy northwest. You can't go back. And would we, older and weathered by the years, like it if we could?

Did Gilpin, I wonder, notice the birds as his coach made its fifteen mile an hour progress? Are we happier for going faster?

I remember, we thought we were, once upon a time. And I do wonder about the young swifts trying out their speedy wings of a summer evening before they leave us for Africa about August 6. In a tight gang – however do they not collide? – they fly as fast as they can, screaming as they bank steeply on the updraughts or – golden memory! – against the sunlit western wall of my College. It must be fun, joy, must it not? But then, think of young men – lads, really – in noisy cars driving too fast, and noisily, with screaming gears, in the evening in Ely's town centre – showing off, as Roy our neighbour says, their little willies. Give or take a bit, not much has changed except the scale: as kids we had to be content with a bit of folded stiff cardboard stuck between a bike frame and the back brake so we could sound like a motorbike – we thought. Speed seemed so glamorous, important. But one day we grow up to other cares. Just as well…

That pace of that rapid 'now you see it, now you don't' glimpse in Michael's car was very much the story of most of my adult life: so much to do, the pressing feeling that you were always trying to catch up with where you ought to have been. Many of our generation felt that. But there comes a time when a sort of wisdom is forced on you, and the gear changes are more careful and you take the corners more carefully: you slowly come to realise that your own sun is westering, that you are moving more slowly when joints are stiffer in the morning, and the tasks around the house and gardens hold less attraction than they did. It is wise not to be too much wedded to staying in a tiny village, however much you love it, when you have to think about a coming time when your eyes will no longer allow you to drive, when what is left of the once excellent bus service is infrequent, unreliable, expensive and teetering on the brink of complete withdrawal 'because we have to provide a sustainable service'.

The walk round the hill and under the dappled spring shade of the wood which the village got together to plant thirty years ago begins to seem a longer way than it used to be. The village shop closed decades ago, killed by affluence and the car. When I first arrived, it had prided itself, hopelessly uneconomically, on stocking everything you could need. (They fell down on Lapsang Souchong, which when we had been undergraduates we thought smart, and so pretended we liked.) The same forces killed other local trades and shops we can now barely remember. The bootmaker from ten miles away no longer came every two months to mend and sell boots, and anyway children stopped wearing the sort of boots covering the ankle with which I had grown up. The knife- and shear-grinder with his bicycle-operated grindstone stopped coming. Our old butcher, Jack Hurrell, long now dead, used to come round the village twice a week in his van with 'Famous Sausages' painted on the back door. He always had titbits for the hopeful, loyal, dogs who drooled after his slow progress, patiently waiting by the door of the van for the scraps he threw to them. He often stopped for a warming whisky in cold weather – but that never affected the accuracy of his cleaver on the chopping block: the blows made the van shake. The baker would also call twice a week with a tray of cakes and fresh bread.

Then there was the big Cambridge-blue van of 'Johnnie Call Weekly'. He came round the villages from Cambridge, and his visit was an Event for some of the lonelier and older folk. He was a little man, twisted up with rheumatism, asymmetric face under a peaked cap with a white top. He remembered their ailments and their families as readily as the small sums they put on tick. He had been coming for years, but his name was never known as any other than that blazoned across the front of his van. The shelves inside his van were separated by a narrow passage just wide enough for him to limp down. They held tinned food, matches, cleaning cloths, candles, wicks for oil lamps, nails, screws, tools, string, needles, thread, rubber sealing rings for Kilner preserving jars, coal shovels, galvanised buckets, soap, scrubbing brushes, brooms. (I still have a shovel, now worn down much shorter than it began, which I bought from him.) At the back of the van a pump dispensed the blue paraffin that many folk still used both for cooking and in round columnar heaters like overgrown top hats. We had two ourselves: wet heat, but heat. All gone now...

These memories of only a few decades ago recall a time and a village inconceivable now even to many whose hair is beginning to grow grey. You can try to tell people about it, but you never can make them feel it. Those memories are of a past that has made me what I can be in what future I have: you cannot leave memories, for those are what make your world twopence coloured rather than blank penny plain. Some baggage accumulated over decades you can't leave behind when you move.

Years ago, Jenny and I remade this house at Reach that it will soon be time gently, graciously, to leave. It was two cheap labourer's cottages run up for £25 or so in 1871, and we loved the hard labour of 'conversion.' (A pity that that word brings religious overtones.) We made this plot blessed with our vegetables and fruits, and hindsight makes it a demi-Eden. (It wasn't: picking frozen sprouts in a wet gale from the north was just as much a part of the reality as the back aching from bending and digging, and hands sore from weeding.) My son and I built the stable where a succession of ponies lived. The sheds – all my building, often from reclaimed wood and things people had thrown out – are full of tools for this and that, tools some of which are smooth from the wear of the hands of the old man who lived across the lane and took my greenness in hand when I first came to this house. I shall probably never need to use them again, but I keep their edges sharp and oiled: just in case. (There is a young man with a family across the lane who might find a use for them...)

The saplings that I planted around the village, in places where tractors could not run over them or sprays reach, are now adults, and spread deep and gracious shade in these hotter summers. If I have done nothing else, I have planted trees. I am on good terms with over 70 of those that survive from my guerrilla planting. But now, as my shadows lengthen, it really is nearly time to stir my stumps and make ready to leave the old house in the village. The consequence is not unhappy: there is the delight of exploring with a mellow, more discerning, excitement another place, another, different, soil to grow things in, a place that you had visited many times before and thought you had known. But you now know you had not even scratched its surface.

On a clear day, looking north and a bit west towards Ely from the top of the hill behind the house in the village, you can see the Cathedral. Once, from that spot, across the marshy fen below you, you would have seen no Octagon, but the huge central tower the Normans built for the building Henry I had made a Cathedral, seat of a new bishopric. (It fell down in 1322.) Before that, you might have seen the smoke from the burning of the Abbey by the Vikings. We fool ourselves if we think that anything, despite any appearance of permanence, lasts.

August – the month I write this, looking out over the garden at Reach – won't let you ignore that fact. The trees look a tired dulled green with all that photosynthesising since the bright hopes of spring. Last August, they were aging faster than usual: it was arguably the hottest for longest this bit of country has ever known. The trees found it hard, for there had been no serious rain since March. We bank, don't we, on the normal. But nothing is normal, even what has always been: Dame Fortune is changeable as the changing moon. That is her normality, constant only in her inconstancy. It was too hot during the day to go outside, to do anything outside – even though much work on the house and garden was needed. Milo lay stretched out wherever in the curtained house he could find a cooler bit of floor. He was out before 6.30 most mornings, on what in normal years one would call a perfect summer morning, flushing the rabbits – he has no hope of catching one – from their feeding in the parched grass, greeting his friends in the community of dogs, reading what passes for dog newspapers from the scents on the grasses and bushes. Full of youth and joy.

Will had combined the wheat on his field that climbs to the top of the hill. In snow, I remember, its westward slope lets you get up a good speed on *langlauf* skis: I wonder if I'll ever do that again? They are still in the shed. To me, a stubble field on a clear summer morning, with the expanse of the Fen behind it, is one of the most beautiful of sights, one which I longed for years ago when caught for days in a failing tent on an Arctic icecap by a serious blizzard – and not sure that we would make it back to the coast and safety. Funny that on a hot morning – the sun, still low, hit you like a blast when you came out of grateful shade – that cold memory, and remembered fear, should have surfaced so keenly... We walked, Milo obediently at heel, to the top of the hill over the soft crunch of the stubble, and stopped. Somewhere beneath our feet was the ghost of – well, what? You can see strange cropmarks, suggestive of some sort of building or structure, on aerial photos. A little further away is a double ring mark, and I'll eat my hat if it is not the ploughed out remains of a Bronze Age barrow. Nothing to be seen on the surface. Sometimes you feel the centuries of men's lives in this little spot of earth pressing in on you, saying 'notice me, don't forget us, we were here before you' almost like the momentary change of light and heat when a cloud passes across the sun. On this field a metal detectorist friend found a silver coin, minted in Egypt by Mark Antony when he was having that fling with Cleopatra. (There was a bit more to it than that, but let that pass.) How did it get to be here? Who, flesh and blood and bone, dropped it and regretted it?

Milo spotted a hare, lying close down, ears flat to its back, a hundred or so yards away downslope, and he was off, oblivious to the whistle. Well, let be: he'll never catch it, and he will learn to be steady as he gets older. He was then only a teenager, and, as Rosanna says, in that stage when, like all young males, he stinks with the sloshing about of so much testosterone, and he couldn't concentrate for long on one thing. (I remember when, decades ago, I was a schoolmaster in a boys' school I insisted on the windows of the room being open all the time whatever the weather. I lost some popularity, particularly among the boys who sat near the winter windows, but the fresh air did dilute the smell, particularly acute after games afternoons, and often made worse by an overlay of Brut.)

But I blew the two short blasts on the whistle, again, and he did answer, and came panting up the slope. Good dog: a treat for that, and we set off down to the spinney in which I planted a couple of dozen trees God knows how many years ago. They are big now, and have pupped. Badgers live there. And rabbits. Milo likes whiffling about in there – we often go back – just as Hector the black Lab used to years ago.

At the edge of the field the combine had left a few square yards of wheat, full in the ear, still standing. It reminded me how in the old days, at harvest, before combines, when the corn was reaped and sheaves stooked, the poor could not go gleaning – and often gleaning produced for them a tidy sack of corn to help through the winter. As long as one sheaf was on the field, no trespass. After it was lifted, the field was open. The women and children – the men would be at work – would move, backs bent, picking up what the reaper had missed, and most farmers said good luck to them. But there were those mean-minded men who would leave a single sheaf there until the winter rains had come from out of the west, and the grain all spoiled and rotting that could have stilled a child's crying for hunger in a thin February.

And so, back to breakfast, along the drove, back to another day of hiding from the heat, typing away in the study with the blinds down, at words nobody may ever read, hoping it will soon go cooler and rain will come, and knowing it won't. For we had weeks of this ahead, I guessed: rightly.

But come the evening, and things were more tolerable. We ate outside, missing the swifts, who had gone off to Africa the previous week, and as the sun dipped to the west told Milo it was time for a walk. The air was still. Just a whiff of honeysuckle as we passed the bush by the shed. Someone had lit a barbecue. A girl's laughter sounded from the trees down by the river – the high laugh of someone still in the morning of their world, when every day is summer. Suddenly Horace's wonderful poem about memories of summer dusks and laughter as he sits with his wine by whitehaired Winter's fire pressed on my memory. I tried to translate it once, and failed to capture it: like trying to hold the moonlight in a net. We walked along the river, the quiet half mile or so towards the spinney, and then the sweep of the stubble up to the fading sky. The west was a glory of purple and orange. From across the river Paul and Jo raised their glasses to us as we passed, and their dogs, two lovely retriever bitches who so loved playing with Milo when he was a puppy, rushed to the edge of their terrace wagging at their teenage heartthrob, who wags back, and then carried on, unconcerned. ('My public, you know...') Somewhere close by – probably in Allan's huge, secret, garden – a muntjac barked its harsh monotonous note. A blackbird called its noisy alarm from the grown-out hedge. I see that a few young sucker elms are trying to come back: they'll make it to the point where their limbs are thick enough for the beetles to move in, alas. Far off, down the Fen, a cock pheasant cried his territorial 'I am going to bed now and this is my perch' call: a young bird, I thought, for he sounds not too certain. Another couple of months and there would be answering calls from all around.

With the light behind us, the stubble was luminous, and my old eyes momentarily saw with a sharpness and intensity I had forgotten. The solitary ash on the skyline stood black against the coming of the night. Then we saw it: first the loom of the rising moon, the full moon of August. Visibly, the face rose, the atmosphere magnifying it so that it looked huge and close. Just for a moment as the lower rim touched the horizon it looked as if it really were a great green cheese about to roll down the sinking skyline of the hill. And then it was clear of the ground and began its ascent to begin its monthly decline. (But that is only how we see it. Who knows how it thinks of itself, its unending partnering of Tellus in this strict dance?) A moment of magic, ever new however often you see it each year, as I have tried to do when this night of the full moon in August is clear. Soon there would be the fullness of the Perseid meteor shower, but with a full moon we did not see much of it.

We walked home in silence, through the darkling wood, Milo busily sniffing his way from anthill to tree bole to fallen branch to things unspeakable. A happy walk. We two, now together, once far apart, have seen many changing moons, as Fortune moved us on from our own bright mornings when the world was all before us and we began the descent, step by unthought step, from our Pisgah sight of what we knew not, to this, a happy, silent, slow walk home with our dog, the dog we are training together, to a last shutting of the doors against the morning's heat, and a book at bedtime.

The black cat from next door ghosted across the road on silent feet, about her mysterious business. I thought of Yeats' Minaloushe the cat, dancing in moonlight, 'lifting to the changing moon his changing eyes.' The early owl calls.

For that evening, that evening light on the stubbles as the inconstant moon begins her dance from light to dark and dark to light, that too is a letting go. In a week's time it was to be 60 years since, a sapling from the other side of England, I first transplanted to this village and grew new roots here. But the view across the fen... Westward and a half north, there Ely lay, and a future that will comprehend the past.

The House in Cow Lane

Ely is as small towns should be – and as indeed were the ones I knew as a boy, like Kendal or Fleetwood. My criteria for a decent town, I might add, are a) an ironmonger, b) a seedsman, c) a good butcher (and preferably two) who hang their beef properly, and compete in the excellence of their sausages and pork pies; d) a good bookshop where you feel the staff might actually read books too, and are ready to chat about anything under the sun, e) a market and a space where people unmolested by cars can, to use the old words, expatiate and confer, as Milton says bees do in front of their new hive.[3] For f), allotments, and, g) if possible, a decent church where they take music seriously. (And, one hopes, religion.) It also ought to be a place where you can feel the past, a long past, nudging the present, where you are aware of the lives of men and women who came before

31

you, who thought so differently, whose world circled a different sun. The little city on a hill has all those things, and a house that when it was new two and a half centuries ago looked across the lane down which the cows went to graze in the common fen to the open fields that would not suffer Enclosure for another half century.

That lane, and others that join it, is shown on John Speed's remarkably accurate map of 1610, which is reproduced on the title page of this book.[4] That house is now jostled and elbowed by the Johnny-come-lately buildings of the town as it has grown over the ancient fields, but is a welcoming place where the folk who have lived there have left happy memory – for I am convinced places hold the memory of people as old clothes keep something of the smell of the men and women who wore them. As the top layer of the palimpsest, the signs of our own handiwork are everywhere – including a quiet enclosed garden where I have made raised beds for my Lady's plantings, and her impeccable taste mellows the summer air with scent. She has planted a *Rosa Banksiae* to ramble its foam of little cream flowers all over the pergola where we park the car. It is a stripling as yet. But not far away, on St Mary's Street, is its relative, an Ancient of Days of roses, clambering all over the front, the dormers, the tiles of the roof of a house that dates from about the same time as the House in Cow Lane. Its main trunk is a good four inches in diameter, its vigour unchecked by the counting of the years.

She has made good choices in her planting, and I hope people we shall never know will look at her rose and be grateful for the froth of beauty each summer.

We saw her Ely house first on a golden September morning. The estate agent's picture had not (really) lied. Outside, it was chocolate box charming. The mellow brick was small, showing it was made before bricks got bigger to avoid the Brick Tax on each brick made and sold. (A bankrupt government had imposed that tax in 1784 to help pay for the American Wars.) On the clay roof tiles moss luxuriated. The lime mortar pointing was neatly penny-rolled, red and white roses climbed and lolled over the windows and reached up to the gutters. In one rose a collared dove had a late nest. Hollyhocks, always such attention-seekers, lolled against the low fence and overhung the pavement. Some were already dropping their many black centred flat seeds as they nudged passers-by.

Inside: well, a lot needed doing, and we could see that straightaway. But the house felt welcoming, kindly, and the ninety-year-old lady who had lived there for sixty-odd years till her death had infused into it an atmosphere of love and care. 'Go through, go and look at the back', said the agent, and that made us realise not only that the house was actually a lot bigger inside than it seemed from the outside, but that there was a lot of usable open space – 'huge potential for development', as they say. We both fell for it, said nothing, and tried, oh so sensibly and dispassionately, to put the other off by itemising the massive job of conversion we would be taking on at a time when many others of our age are thinking of – well, whatever it is that people do in retirement. But each of us was thinking, 'Look no further.'

Well, she bought it. Work, and a lot of labouring that made me remember muscles I had long forgotten. Item, a lot of demolition and stripping out, which I do thoroughly enjoy. Item: central heating, which meant the pamment floor in what would be the dining room had to come up – damp as hell anyway. Item: new kitchen where the old milking parlour had been, for which Rosanna splashed out on a hugely self-indulgent but beautiful counter of green Honister slate – not slate at all, but metamorphosed tuff – to remind us of a corner of England we both love. Item: reconstruct the outside privy as a laundry room - cubby hole, really – and re-roof with new wood and the old pantiles which I had handled carefully so as to preserve the houseleeks that adorned them.

That was a happy job, finished one long summer afternoon with grandson Willem. Item: rip out the defunct 1930s tiled fireplace – heavy brute! – in the parlour – and find behind its rubbish infill a graceful eighteenth century alcove into which a woodburner would neatly fit. Item – the big one: first, clearing their clutter from the range of three garages, all that was left of the original barn the roof of which blew off in the Great Storm of 1987. Much of the clutter was in the 'that will come in' category: lots of usable timber; a barrel of creosote; various half used pots of paint; a Victorian cast iron mortice cutter weighing a couple of hundredweight, now a stern backdrop to the frivolous luxuriance of the asparagus bed; and 3,264 bricks, stacked neatly along the wall, which Rosanna's son and I moved out one hot June day. (They became the garden wall.) The erstwhile garages have become a library, a treatment room for Rosanna (she is an acupuncturist), and a guest annexe, but not before weeks of me, alone but for Radio 3, lining them, walls, floor, ceiling with insulation, and wiring them, and plaster boarding, and so on. Then, after that big job, there was only the small matter of a walled garden… and a little matter of 2,487 old clay tiles to be moved from under an ancient and bad tempered bramble bush.

We were courteous to the shades of those who had been there before us, but they had left few traces. Though we know there was some sort of Roman activity only fifty yards away, we found no archaeology in the trenches dug for the drains even though Speed's map shows there was some sort of building on that spot even then. (I do wonder about the base of one of the side walls, which untypically of the house has Barnack ragstone in it, and is not keyed into the bricks.) There was nothing under the floors – though the lady's sons, Roy and Maurice, told us that when they had laid a new concrete floor in one room they found tiles 'just like those in the Cathedral…' 'What did you do with them?' 'Oh, we put them in the concrete mixer…' There were just a few recoverable and presentable scraps of the early nineteenth century stencilling on the parlour walls: that had done duty for the more expensive wallpaper of that period. But we could feel that there had been kindly people there for a long, long time.

Uncovering a large void that had been deliberately made (why?) on the landing of the stairs, we found a woman's right shoe, dateable to the 1940s – shoes in this part of England were sometimes deposited 'for luck'. There was a Woodbine cigarette packet, and a *Cambridge Evening News* of 1963 with a story that the H-bomb might be used to dig a new Panama Canal. Given the madness of now, it seemed to recall a time of relative innocence…

Any old house is layered with people's stories, now unknowable, and we are adding our script to it, of course.

One can so easily be tedious about something which is of small interest to those who have not hewn its wood and got its cement under their fingernails, and tired their hands with the stubbornness of cables and sockets. But I look round the place, as I do at the old house by the stream in the village, which I shall leave to my children, and I remember the work, and the satisfied tiredness, and the taste of a beer at the end of a day when it had gone well. And I think I have got better, over the years, as a craftsman, and the old ones would not be too displeased with what we have done. Years ago, in that house in the village, I took out a window and built in a new one. I finished off round it with Polyfilla, decorated, and thought no more about it. Then, much, much later, that room had to be redecorated, and under the wallpaper, scratched into the Polyfilla when it had been wet was the remark, 'Dad is a very messy painter.' My son's estimate was accurate enough; but what, I wonder, will some future owner speculate about that? It is disconcerting enough to see ourselves as we were seen by our children before the age of discretion. So I am glad my son's son and I have worked together even if only on the roof of what was a privy in the house at Ely, and that we did a good job.

And, speaking of which: at Reach it was my ideas that made the template for what we did, and they were not always good ones. More than once, later, when we had learned a lot more, I found myself cursing my earlier work for being too strong in concrete or, bluntly, bodged, and having to redo it to a better plan. But in Her House, it was her choice that carried weight, as was only right. Many a time she would suggest something, and I would shake my head and say, 'No, that won't work', only to find

36

when I had done it that it did. It was rather a pleasant experience to be Lieutenant rather than Captain, for a change. If something was awkward, it wasn't my fault; if something worked well, smiles all round.

But she can't mix decent mortar and has strange ideas about what you can make water do.

The collared doves bring off usually three broods a year in the roses above the door, above the Westmorland slate panel in which I carved the number of the house. In the jasmine that clambers along the kitchen wall in the courtyard towards the back door, a bright-eyed blackbird has her nest in season, just above my head height, and she sits immobile, her beak lifted slightly above the horizontal, as I say 'Good Morning' to her as I walk past. From our bedroom, occasionally, we see one of the peregrines that patronise the Cathedral dart past, and a clatter of alarmed pigeons. On the ridge of the roof in the next garden there are usually three pigeons, engaging in some complicated *ménage à trois*. In the garden the apple trees have borne their first fruit, and the birch My Lady planted, the birch that reminds her of childhood, and her Russian grandmother's love of that tree, is growing straight and tall. Strange: the first tree I planted at the Reach house by the stream was also a birch, planted the month my daughter was born. The wheel turns, be it morning or evening.

Rosanna has been delighted with a new app for her phone: Merlin Bird ID, which can tell you what birds you are hearing. She often wakes early, and in the dawns of May switches on the app to identify who is helping out this morning with the annual miracle of the Spring dawn chorus. The other morning, bright, with a bit of low mist, the promise of heat later, she woke, got up, and went to the open window next door that looks out eastwards towards the Cathedral – still a joy to see that silhouetted against the lightening sky. The app told her: blackcap, robin, wren, collared dove, house sparrow, wood pigeon (of course!), great tit, chiffchaff. And bittern. When I woke later, she told me of the app's recognition of that low boom. Well, we know that bittern are breeding at Roswell Pits, and the sound – which will carry a long way, and the bittern is apparently the loudest British bird – could just about have reached our open window. Both of us were delighted.

A week or so later we are at the village. Again I sleep, again she wakes, and goes to the bathroom, the window of which looks out over the trees of the garden and the fen beyond. (There is noticeably more of a chorus on that side, rather than the street side, of the house.) She switches on the app. Roughly the same tally – but a bittern? (Admittedly, the clever app had suggested it was not quite sure.) When she told me, I wondered if one had been heard in Wicken Fen Nature Reserve, but that is a good two miles away. The same thing happened the next morning, and I began to think about going over to Wicken to ask if bitterns had been reported.

But then, the third morning, she is again in the bathroom, I am again asleep, and she notices that the low booming shows in the sound trace on the app. The spikes coincide with a – very gentlemanly, quite quiet, you understand – rhythmic rumble from the bedroom where I am sleeping the sleep of the just.

I have not checked the records at Wicken.

Rosanna grew up in Ealing, where, as in all towns there are certain things taken for granted, like buses and traffic, shops, background noise, pavements – and that most people you pass in the street will be strangers. Her House in Cow Lane is also in a town, though a small one: engaging with this, and with learning to live there, is a new experience for me, peasant through and through. How do you get to know a place you always 'knew', but never knew? If you are like me, you might seek out what I call its ghosts: the stories and traces of the people who have been there before us. For the past is not dead: it isn't even over. The drawback to doing what I do is that while amusing yourself you can rapidly become tedious to others, and (for me) it is always well to keep in mind that, as Rosanna and others have warned me, sometimes the more you know the less you see. You encounter your knowledge, not the thing itself. How often I have fallen into that trap! And I am sure I shall again in this book.

Even so, I do think it is a great help to have an idea of a place as a historical palimpsest, to think what it might have been like actually to have been, for example, the Princess Etheldreda, who in 673 founded the first monastery, not far from where the House in Cow Lane would one day stand. For when in the place where you settle a lot has happened in local, national and international history, and you don't yet know many of your new neighbours whom you did not choose (nor they you), it's the people who came before us whose shades populate the streets and fields that once they knew. And of course, once you know about them, they won't go away. They were as real, as contradictory and confused as we are. They enjoyed good company, they got colds and tummy bugs like we do, and they faced the same puzzle of existence as we do. Sometimes you hear (you think) their voices. Gradually, though, living people do come into focus: the people you meet at the allotment and with whom you share grumbles about the weather, and then (often deep) conversations on the state of the world as you both lean on your hoe, grateful for the rest; as ever, fellow dog walkers whose dog's names you know before you know theirs; and people at the Cathedral or selling things on the market – the four things, in essence, that ultimately hold communities together, however remote they seem: the labour and cycles of the land, animals and their management, exchange, and the customs and rituals of religion. Be that as it may: at the start you know few people, and if you walk down the street and talk to everyone you meet, as I would when walking round the village, in a town people start looking at you strangely. I have always done it, and the habit is hard to break, even if it embarrasses Rosanna when she is with me. But a dog is a help: they have no human inhibitions, and Milo has already made friends with, among others, a black Lab bitch who lives nearby and her owners have been round for a drink and much conversation on areas, serendipitously, of common interest and expertise.

There are, too, parts of the town where you are reminded that the countryside and its culture waits not far away. In season the rich odour of fresh cowpats flavours the breeze as you enjoy the view of the Cathedral from Dean's Meadow where Red Dexter cattle graze. By the river, avoiding the Lycra-clad joggers, you might meet men and women in sensible, battered tweeds with whistles on lanyards and happy spaniels and Labradors. Or you might be greeted by a young and eager Lab in Cherry Hill Park, in the interim of being put through his training paces by a man in a Barbour and Le Chameau gumboots that had seen much service. (His smug little spaniel sat at the man's feet, obviously waiting for the young hooligan to make a mess of things…)

Then, once, at the end of Spring Head Lane, where the water of Roswell Pits reflected the winter sunset behind Rosanna and me, an elderly spaniel was happily remembering her lost youth with a gentle, slow, bit of retrieving. Her elderly owner had thrown a dummy into the field in memory of other days. As he bent to take it from her I recognised that he too creaked a bit, as I now do. It was dusk (her gloaming too), and her owner and we shared the memory of the pain brought by loss of a loved dog, who in the field has been almost your second self.

Training a working dog is a pleasure, and challenge, that you just have to share. You don't rule your dog: you converse with it. And the best lesson about dog training I was ever given was when Hector of dear memory, then young to the game, was apparently refusing to obey me in the fields I knew as a youth, and my elderly neighbour said, 'Trust your dog: they have noses. You don't'. True enough: and over the drystone wall he went, to come back with a cock pheasant in his mouth that all the other dogs had missed.

That elderly bitch and her slow retrieve underlined how, as you get older, some things you still care about come to matter in a different way. Like shooting. As a boy, when people had been shooting nearby I used to find the odd spent 12bore cartridge case – usually one of the red Eley ones, in paper cases with a brass bottom – and I would treasure the useless thing for days as if somehow it could magically make me part of that world. It was the nearest I could get to a gun and the country (not county!) world I so wanted fully to belong to. In my 20s I was so proud of my first 12-gauge shotgun, a dreadful, indeed dangerous, superannuated hammer gun, without safety catch, made about 1890. Seth had sold it to me for £10: it was his spare gun which he had given up using. (Wise man...) I was even prouder when with it I began to hit things that fed the family – and times were not easy for us. (But both barrels tended to go off at once, which could be disconcerting, and hard on the shoulder.) Over the years I developed into quite a decent shot. I got a safer gun, taught my son, who became (and is) an excellent shot who in time captained the Cambridge University Clay Pigeon team. He bought himself a really good gun when he could afford it, and gave me the comfortable, no frills, Belgian farmer's workaday side-by-side I had bought for £100 from a friend for him when he was 14. I came to shoot with that in preference to my others, even on the odd quite smart shoot to which I was invited. For I could consistently hit things with it, sometimes better than my smarter neighbours on the next pegs.

There was one man, half a generation older than me, on the cooperative shoot I was eventually – it is a long story – invited to join and where I shot for over 20 years. We shot in the sweet country of the Lune valley in the north country I still think of as home. He was a very good shot indeed, elegant and economical in movement: not much got past him, even when he had lost the sight of one eye. His joy was warming to see when his grandsons started learning the ways of the countryside, and graduated from model shotguns they self-importantly carried in the correct safety-conscious manner to shooting with him, using the very same .410 bore on which his own father had taught him. But there came a point when he turned up at the meet without his gun. There was the usual flurry of greetings, pegs being drawn, excited, self-important dogs – 'This is work, you know, not just fun!' – milling around, and I quietly asked Tom why no gun. 'I have killed enough birds in my life, Charles, and killed them cleanly. I no longer want to. But I love this bit of countryside and the sport, and the skill it takes to take a high fast bird without his knowing about it, and I shall keep coming. It is my grandsons' turn now.' Dear Tom, on him be peace.

And that feeling came to me too, a few years later. Over the years I had had quite a few days when I had been top gun, I had had the odd occasion when everything went right. (Once, a vanishingly high, screamingly fast pheasant fell stone dead almost on the back of my beloved Hector, eager at my side. No work for him on that one: he did not even have to pick it up.) When Milo arrived, we decided that he should be trained as a gundog, for Labradors are bred for that. It is in their genes, and they love the work. He was a natural: and there are few joys to compare with getting to the point where the silent communication by look and gesture can make you and your dog a team. So Milo had intensive basic training in the garden with me, and then, although he had already worked half a season quite well, went with me to Big School with two gifted ladies who not only simply loved dogs but also were experienced trainers of gundogs. He loves the work, and a distant motorcycle backfiring will have him on his feet, ears cocked, looking eagerly at the sky for something to fall.

But this last couple of seasons I realised I felt like Tom: I had had enough hot blood on my hands. I love the skill, I loved the way we friends respected our quarry, even (privately, some of us) thanked it, and shared out the bag fairly for our tables at the end of the day. (We were not, as they say, in the numbers game.) So I decided to stop regular shooting. Being competitive, even against myself, no longer mattered. I would keep the gun for the occasional attempt at keeping the population of the (delicious) woodpigeons down – they are prolific and promiscuous breeders and can wreck your vegetable garden, which matters to me, in ten minutes – and we would simply go to see our friends in the country I love, with Milo to pick up the birds that are not missed. It was a big step, but less steep than I thought it would be for me when Tom first told me his thoughts.

Milo does not mind that on the hill I no longer carry a gun – though he looks eager if I do go to the gun safe to get one of the important documents we stuff away there. On the hill he has friends to meet and work to do, and retires at the end of the day happy, exhausted: 'This is what I was made to do.' A dog's life is so much less complicated – so far as we know! – than ours. He happily inhabits two quite different worlds, the delights of the town and the open fell and the secret woods that line the ghylls.

Two of my grandchildren, both countryfolk, are very fine shots. They will inherit my guns, among them the folding .410 poacher's gun on which I taught myself to shoot.

The talents of dogs… scent hounds, sight hounds, once all connected with their usefulness to man. The greyhound, like its cousin the alaunt, was once a fierce beast, bred for running down the fast and fierce wild boar, as the name suggests – *gris*, as in place names like Grisdale.

A last ember of that culture still glows in hare coursing, rightly now illegal, but still common enough. And the dogs are treated pretty badly, disposable once their fleetness begins to leave them. The same is true of commercial greyhound racing: hence the number of retired greyhounds one meets, who always look mildly vacant and never seem to enjoy things much. Perhaps their joints hurt. But I met a chap with a black one by the river early one morning – or rather Milo did, and unusually the hound reciprocated his interest, and wagged its tail, and I asked if it was retired from the track. 'Never made it,' said his human, in a strong Norfolk accent. 'He's cross eyed: couldn't see the hare when the traps opened. So they were going to have him put down, but I got there first.' Lucky dog. Others are not. I gave him a biscuit, and he took it in his long jaws gravely, politely, with what looked like pleasure.

A thought: our two species have been together so long that one does wonder who domesticated whom in this mutual usefulness. Did our scenting ability atrophy because our dogs did it for us, and did they lose their colour vision – they still have the remnants of the structures in their brains – and sharpness of sight because we did that for them? And then, man breeds that sight back as in greyhounds?

Of course I admit I find town walks (unless I am being antiquarian) much less attractive than having grass and soil under my feet, and long views to draw my eyes forward. I easily get fed up with nosily looking into the same gardens, the same lighted windows, seeing the same blue flicker of TV screens on evening curtains. Dogs probably don't get fed up with the same walk time after time, for, after all, the smellscape will be quite different. But their humans, like me, do get restive, and need fresh things to look at – or, at least, known things at a different stage of the season or in different weather. Also, when you are getting to know, somewhat shyly, a new place where nobody knows you, walking the dog is as good an excuse as any for wandering about, or loitering without intent: you are not just a strange and possibly suspicious character in gumboots leaning on a cromach but a man who fits into an identifiable and reassuring category. Or so I hope, but will never find out.

So, kill two birds with one stone: find a new walk where the dog's feet will not be always on pavement, and fill in a bit more of the jigsawed palimpsest of layered time. The morning promised much rain later as he and I set off to find St Audrey's Well: 'Etheldreda' can soon wear down on the tongue to 'Audrey.'

A story, traceable back to the 12th century (500 and more years after she died), says a healing spring rose when her sister and successor as Abbess, Seaxburh, moved Etheldreda's uncorrupted body from her first grave to a new one. Only recently dead, her grave had attracted the veneration of pilgrims as they had sought her counsel when alive. (The preservation of her body was taken as confirmation of her sainthood.) Tradition says that first burial was somewhere near St Mary's Church – pretty near the area of highest ground, which might well have been the site of her first foundation, the church and abbey which the Vikings of the Great Heathen Army burned in 870.* That was a couple of hundred metres west of the present Cathedral, and indeed there is some archaeological evidence for a spring near there whose stream ran down what is now a dry valley to the river. But to have cut that valley any stream would have needed many more centuries than those since Etheldreda's death. And the dog needs a longer walk than that.

So on we go, down past the (in the circumstances) happily named Fountain pub – the road it stands on was called Fountain Lane many moons ago – to the old main gate Prior Walpole built for the Abbey after 1396. Past the old Theological College and the basketball courts of

---

* Jeremy Harte: *English Holy Wells: a Sourcebook* (Heart of Albion Press, 2008), Vol.2, p.176-7.

the King's School, and we pick up the footpath across the golf course that leads eventually, after a couple of miles, to a grange on the fen-edge at Braham by Little Thetford. There was a Bronze Age crossing of the river there (when the fens were much less wet than they later became), and the monks of the grange supplied the monastery with the fen's riches in fish and fowl. They might well have come this way, for all over England many footpaths are very ancient, long before they are first marked on the newfangled Ordnance Survey maps that came in with the Napoleonic scare.

I have to watch the dog here, and not be overconfident of his good manners, for, walking across another course, he once ignored my furious recall whistle and happily retrieved a golf ball to a hugely embarrassed me from its place on the smooth green of the hole, with skid marks where he had come to a halt to pick it up. The owner took it from me without a word. The dog could not care less about evidence of the water trade in the canal cut to the river, except to plunge into it and emerge happily muddy and a bit more pungent. But he has found a pool, also somewhat muddy, fringed by willow and scrub, and is happily paddling in and lapping up what is almost certainly the spring and pool named as 'St Aldreth's Well' – say it quickly and it is a pardonable error for a busy engraver – on Sir Jonas Moore's *Mapp of the Great Levell of the Fenns* (London, for Moses Pitt, 1685)*. If this be indeed the well of health-giving and healing water mentioned by Gregory of Ely in the 12th century, well,

---

* Moore was Surveyor to the Earl of Bedford's Company for the draining of the Fens – and many other things, including being an early FRS. He died in 1679.

drink on, and take your fill, even if you are extraordinarily muddy. I'll pass on that for the moment. Breakfast calls. And the rain is starting. But we'll add this one to the list of decent walks.

And that pause by the pool, idly watching the dog, was midwife to a thought, which turned into an idea, which turned into a book: what was Etheldreda's world like?* What was she like? You can read it if you like. Having written that book, she won't leave me now, and under the face of the modern city the bones of her world nag at me: remember us. Remember when the House in Cow Lane was not there.

One problem of moving is your sheds. 'You can never have enough sheds', old Seth said to me when at Reach I was building my first (still standing, still useful) out of old aircraft crates begged from Marshalls Aerospace (they did not call it that then) at the airport. That one served – serves – me well. But give a few years, and daughter gets a pony, and that shed is far too small for a stable, so my son and I build a stable with a tack room and a small hayloft. Then we start making our own hay off the droves round the village and we need somewhere to store it, so we build a sort of open annexe to shed no. 1. But hay means the bikes can't go where they used to, so a small bike shed appears. By this time, too, we have gone in seriously for woodburning stoves, and so we need a place near the house to store at least a couple of tons

---

* *Etheldreda's World: Princess, Abbess, Saint* (Merlin Unwin, 2023)

of logs. Then a large chest freezer appears, and exercise equipment, and filing cabinets (which breed when you are not watching), so *that* woodshed comes down to be replaced by something much more substantial. It was still built with reclaimed materials – old habits die hard – and I was particularly happy to be able to roof it in old clay pantiles that had been sitting around growing moss at the bottom of the garden for thirty years or so. They came off a lean-to shed at the side of the house that we demolished forty years ago to make a garage. But another woodshed has to be built on the other side of the garden… (Better make it a bit bigger this time…) You see, countryfolk got used to wasting nothing, throwing nothing away that might conceivably be useful. When David, whose black Labrador and our yellow Milo are friends, was farming in Essex, one of his men bent down and picked up a bent washer in the yard. 'What do you want that for?', says David. 'Well, boss, happen I don't need it now, but if I ever does I'll have un handy, like.' (How times change: he remembers giving the men working for him in the fields a daily allowance of beer.)[5]

And then, as the unrelenting years pass, this downsizing business becomes a real issue… where is everything going to go? Well, of course, it won't fit into the House in Cow Lane: some of it you will never use again, like the big two-handed saw – lovely steel! – for cutting clunch from the quarries up the hill that Seth gave me, or the hedge slashers kept sharp, oiled and masked, ready for the use they will never now get from me… I never laid a hedge well, but at least I tried. It's all got to go. Well, as well as an attitude Seth did give me a lot of his old tools as he grew older, so I could pass on those tools to my neighbours, young Luke or Jonathan, who both have families to keep and hearts that love tools even if they are used only once in a blue moon. I suspect a lot of what Seth gave me had come to him in the same way, accepted with the same readiness because 'it will come in one day.' (I never had to saw up clunch. But I might have done.) But I shall keep the handsaw he gave me, and the sawset to set the blade when you have filed it sharp with the triangular file. 'Set 'er proper, bor, should be able to run a needle down between them teeth.' He taught me a lot, but he was a hard teacher, and was not satisfied with much less than perfection. A needle could indeed run down the teeth of my sharpened saw.

It was hard, but I became quite friendly with the men at the new Recycling Centre (aka dump) on my frequent visits. Admittedly, at much of the cherished stuff I took they shook their heads, and put it in the landfill skip, but they took quite a bit for selling on. They did have quite a selection of stuff, and I could not in all conscience not browse… and buy occasionally. That's when they started calling me 'mate'.

When the House in Cow Lane was finished and the garden laid out, there was only one thing that was missing. So I built a shed, a beauty. One of the old six-paned windows that I had taken out years back from the house at Reach gave daylight to the workbench, and the 1950s light globe from Reach's kitchen lit up its darkness.

But it is too small…

Waterland

So here we are, living half the week in this new/old place, which we have to get to know in a wholly new way. I shall never know it in the way I know Reach, with the salt sweat of my youthful brow sometimes making the eyes of old age blink. But there are other ways, just as valuable, of knowing, just as new love when you are old differs from but is not less valuable than that first fine careless rapture (I do like clichés) that was such pleasing pain and painful pleasure in our thoughtless springs.

Back, as they say, to basics. I can be quite geeky – a word my grandchildren use, which I like – about some things. For example, I cannot help thinking of landscape as something unstable, dynamic, in constant change, a sort of palimpsest where you can read, or picture in your mind – like taking filters off one by one – what it once was, glimpse another time – and even what it might be again. This is a passion that Rosanna, a historical geographer by academic persuasion if an acupuncturist by trade, and I share, and it makes time fly on many a car journey. Take, for example, the Lakes, a bit of England I love and know very well indeed. You look at it now, and it is so easy to think it has always been like it is, that mix of high bare fell where the agile sheep graze, and woods in the valleys and on some hillsides, and the pretty whitewashed farms.

But look closer, and you realise that, oddly, very few of the trees are really old – and trees can live a very long time. (But there is a magnificent Yew – it deserves a capital letter – that stands in Martindale churchyard which is at least 1300 years old, and like Johnny Walker still going strong.) When John Constable painted Keswick in 1807, there were hardly any trees except on the islands in the lake. For what people now travel miles to see is a post-industrial site, where the trees have reclaimed the ground lost when their ancestors in the original old forest, covering all the land before man came, were felled for charcoal to fire the bloomeries. (Yes, you can find traces of them too, level grass covered spaces, if you know where and how to look.) There the lead ore, and the copper, and a tiny bit of gold, were smelted. The valleys in the time of the first Elizabeth would have been loud with her German miners – the locals called them 'Dutchies' - blasting their way into the rock with gunpowder, and working their water-powered trip hammers, and in still weather smoke from the furnaces would put a blue-grey blanket over the valleys. There is only one tiny bit of the original oak forest left: high up in Keskadale, below the long ridge of Ard Crags that ends in Aikin Knott and its burial cairn.

Hardly anybody goes to that little wood unless they love and revere trees. But the ranging sheep eat so many of the oaklings, and the young tender rowans, and the tasty hawthorns, and as long as they range on the hills the Old Forest will not be reborn. Remove the sheep from the hills – which might happen with the current pressures on hill farming – and in ten years, young woodland would be reaching up to the sun each spring. Nothing is constant.

So too with the Fens, the landscape most altered, recently, by man, perhaps, in the whole of England. Long, long before there was mankind on this planet, Gaia was trying first one thing, then another. Way, way back, tropical seas full of strange life were laying down what is beneath our careless feet. Some 155 million years ago, in the Jurassic, those warm seas laid down here the oldest, underlying layer, the Ampthill Clay. The younger Kimmeridge Clay (also Jurassic), lies on top of that layer, and it runs right under England from the sea-nibbled coast and the oil wells of Dorset out to Doggerland, lost once more beneath the waves that once made it. It is full of fossils of marine creatures, from tiny ammonites to fearsome plesiosaurs – which I have never found, alas, though my neighbour Colin Washtell did find a bit of one, years and years ago. (But Mary Anning got there first – a remarkable woman: she sold sea shells on the sea shore.)

Imagine a time, much more recent – only 160,000 years ago – when from the vast icy blanket that stretched up over Scandinavia, a tongue of ice that had licked down to cover where the Fens now are began its slow retreat. It left a layer of rubbly rubbish chewed out of the land by the ice. Headlong meltwater rivers (which slowed when the sun went down and the temperature dropped) ran through the bared land, leaving banks of gravels, and sand: you can find them on the higher bits of the fens. At that time, at the end of the last ice age some 11,000 years ago, the ancestors of the Trent and Ouse and Nene and Welland and Cam and all the other rivers of Eastern England, now so slow and usually tame, were roaring, wide torrents wearing away the soft land into spacious valleys and terraces. The modern rivers are now only effete shadows, dribbles, of what they once were. But don't ignore them: they can still have a way of being awkward.

We have already got into new habits for a new house and town in the five years since Rosanna found the house. One is walking with Milo down to the quiet river, for he loves water. Getting accustomed to walking in a town takes time, certainly for a young, country-bred Labrador, let alone for dyed in the wool old me. For him not every day now is it happily straight out of the back door and onto the drove, or up the hill to the wood. A quarter of a mile of hard pavement, cars going past, many informative lamp posts, and much, much sniffing to be negotiated before he gets to the first grass in front of the Cathedral. (Sometimes I like to try to imagine what the world looks like from his height – not by getting down to it in public, you understand. But of course his eyes do not work like ours.) For him the Russian cannon captured in the Crimean War in front of the Cathedral is simply a sort of super lamp post. (But not for us: in February 2022 someone dressed it in Ukraine's colours, and put flowers in its muzzle – a bitter reminder of 1968, when the Czechs could not fight the invading Russians but instead stood in front of the tanks, with some putting *flowers* in the soldiers' hair and in the gun muzzles.)

Then we may go round the east end of the Cathedral, past the Dean's Meadow, skirting the mown undulations that are all that remains of the Norman motte and bailey, and down to the river. Milo likes that stretch, for he often meets doggy friends and, if they (and their owners) are willing, can have a romp with them. But sometimes we take the longer route down the steep slope of Fore Hill to the ancient, tree-shaded lane that ends at the level crossing over the busy railway and the quiet waters of Roswell Pits. (In 1877 Skertchley in his *Geology of the Fenland* calls them 'Roslin Hole'.) After that, it's a mere step to the flood plain and the river where there is no taming quay or paved path. Half a mile from the centre of the city, and the world is quiet, and (if you look in the right directions) you hardly see a building. In season slow-eyed, wet-muzzled stock graze there, knee deep in the rich sward. Sweet-smelling splodges of dung spatter the path. (When there was still a milking herd in the village, Ernie's cows on their way to and from milking used to drop in the lane by the house, and I shovelled it up as manure for my tomatoes. But I have not yet got as familiar with the town and its ways as to do that now.) Near the centre as it is, this place and its wetland have a secret life untroubled by people passing along the path. Once, years ago, a friend of mine, looking out from an early train to Manchester that runs on its embankment across the meadow where there used to be watercress beds, saw a red deer stag standing thoughtfully by the distant hedge. The rare bittern has been heard enjoying a welcome boom. (Chaucer's word is better: a bittern 'bombleth in the mire.') We go down to the water, so that Milo can swim, an activity at which he excels, to the consternation of the great crested grebes, who look so surprised, and the annoyance of the geese, and the indignation of the bad-tempered swans. (Last week we saw Mr and Mrs Great Crested Grebe – the sexes are almost impossible to tell apart if you are not a grebe – proudly escorting, one on each side, their two offspring.) An early sculler may glide past, lost in the graceful effort of good oarsmanship, or a pair in rhythmic harmony, and sometimes if we are really early even the Blue Boat or *Goldie*: for Cambridge University Boat Club have built a new boathouse on the other bank so that they can get ready for the Tideway on a larger stretch of quiet water than the Cam can offer. Milo, when very young and first confident of water, showed every sign of wanting to retrieve, or at least swim alongside, an elegant shell that was gliding past…

'Down by the Riverside'…That riverside means so many different things to different people. By the bank, just opposite the new boathouse, there are some majestic bramble bushes who have (as is their wont) reached out and taken fresh grip on the nurturing earth. And again, and again, growing, spreading, spreading, and you never know what you will find, animal or vegetable, in the sheltering microclimates of those rich habitats. Between them and the river there are secluded patches of grass, close nibbled by the geese, lovely quiet places where you can catch the morning sun or dream away a languorous afternoon – as fishermen do, catching little except the glint of light on the river. Milo, uncouth as he is, loves to barge round the brambles and plunge into the water, and then gruntingly haul himself out and shake copiously over anything and anybody nearby. Usually near there we check him in case there should be fishermen who don't value the disturbance and muddying of the water a plunging Labrador can cause.

One July, late afternoon, we were walking along the river. Everywhere was quiet: one of those rare days when the world seems to be holding its breath, for the slight east wind carried any noise of traffic on the Soham road away from us as we walked. By common, silent, consent, we thought he deserved a swim on so hot an afternoon, so meandered towards the bramble screen, deep in our thoughts. Milo ran ahead, and waited expectantly, looking back at us from the fringe of reeds. Then he stopped looking at us, turned abruptly to his right, and wagging his tail furiously and happily, dashed behind the brambles. There was a noise clearly of some consternation. We came to the bank, to find two very young men in swimming trunks and two very young girls in bikinis, who had clearly been enjoying some takeaway food and some cans of beer and perhaps improving conversation. They got up confusedly from the towels on which they had been sitting to shoo a very happy Milo away from their takeaway containers. Their idyll had been rudely disturbed, as only a singleminded dog can do, and we made his excuses as best we could – but what could one say? – and left. At least he did not plunge in and then shower them with his happy shaking on rising from the waves.

It was a curiously touching moment. I suppose it was the (shall I call it innocence?) of that – well, not quite idyll, not quite un *Déjeuner sur l'Herbe*, not quite Seurat's *La Grande Jatte* – and the happiness of those two lads and two lasses just beginning their dance to the music to Time, as we are – I am – coming into the last set of ours… We were the observers, chorus to their actors, as we were once the observed, to whom anyone over twenty was invisible. I hope our younger selves were observed, raw and silly as we were, with the benevolence that the vulnerability of the young elicits in me – yes, I know they are awful as well, but so was I, silly, stupid, selfish. (I do hope the years have improved me, but who am I to say?) My mind flashed back to Thomas Gray's *Ode on a Distant Prospect of Eton College*, so readily appropriated:

> *Say, Father [Ouse], for thou hast seen*
> *Full many a sprightly race*
> *Disporting on thy margent green*
> *The paths of pleasure trace,*
> *Who foremost now delight to cleave*
> *With pliant arm thy glassy wave?*

But

> *Alas, regardless of their doom,*
> *The little victims play!*
> *No sense have they of ills to come,*
> *Nor care beyond to-day:*
> *Yet see how all around 'em wait*
> *The ministers of human fate,*
> *And black Misfortune's baleful train!*

> *…Where ignorance is bliss, 'tis Folly to be wise.*

And I found myself calling down a blessing on those four young folk, happy on a summer afternoon, whom I shall never see again.

And the background music for this pastoral? Not, perhaps, in this case, *L'Après-midi d'un Faune.* Might the post-American Civil War spiritual we sang in our '60s youth serve? 'Gonna lay down my burden/Down by the riverside/ I ain't gonna study war no more.' If only...

I love wetlands, marginal places, places of becoming – just as I loved the marshes and mosses of the Lancashire coast of my youth. Within sight of the Cathedral and a hop, skip and jump from Sainsbury's, in season long-billed wintering birds probe the rich mud of the flood plain, and geese, just flown in from their strenuous summer in the far northlands, quietly and busily graze. One is always on guard, head up, watchful, and they take the job in turns. They suddenly break out a chorus of honks, and apparently for no reason at all will take off, and fly round, and come back. (Geese have a gut with remarkably rapid throughput. They defecate, copiously, when they take off too – I suppose to lose weight. Which is why their visits to Cambridge's velvety College riverside lawns are not welcome.)

I like geese: we kept them years ago, six white Emdens, intelligent – indeed cunning, especially about getting out and wandering all over the village – creatures with innocent forget-me-not blue eyes. As they grazed in the garden or next door's orchard, they would always call to the migrating autumn skeins as they flew over, and were sometimes answered. No chance of having geese again in the House in Cow Lane, alas, but it is almost as good to watch the March courtship of a pair of greylags on the wash at Ely, to guess from the pattern of His Lordship's patrolling where she is sitting, and to see them in the first warm sunshine of the year proudly escorting their four downy hatchlings in a tight bunch along the river. (They are instantly alert when they see Milo, but he will not attempt to retrieve them unless I tell him. And I shall not.) It's good: but not quite as good as them getting to know you and coming to my call, as the Emdens did.

Once, only a century or so ago, this river would have been no place for the delicate eights and fours, or the dull chugging of pleasure cruisers as graceful as overgrown soap dishes. It and its tributaries, including the now almost deserted Lode up to the important port of Reach, were busy with commercial traffic. In the winter season strings of lighters full of sugar beet would be being towed by smoky steam tugs to Ely Sugar Beet Factory. There might even be one or two barges, if the wind was right, under sail, either a big square sail like that of the Norfolk wherry with the gaff as least as long as its boom, or a simple loose-footed lug.

We often spend time near Roswell Pits. They too used to be far from the quiet place they are now, disturbed only by the dinghies of the sailing club, and the calls of waterfowl and in season the harsh Kria! Kri-ia! call of the Little Terns that nest on the artificial islands. (They range widely: I have seen one fishing on Reach Lode. And that call sends shivers down both our spines, while memories of watching their larger cousins nesting in the High Arctic we both love momentarily occlude the soft, leafy world around us.) Many folk see the Pits simply as a nature reserve, a secretive place to sit and fish, or just quietly to sit and contemplate mortality. It is so easy to forget they are entirely man-made, like the flooded peat diggings that made the Broads of Norfolk. The labour of men with pick and shovel dug this great hole.

Shallow water filled the diggings. Then reeds grew, which were harvested each winter for thatching and matting. The pits were full of fish, and early in the 1900s at least one couple, Paul and Sally Gotobed, made a living netting fish and catching eels in the Pits: he made his own grigs of osier for catching the eels. They sold their catch fresh in the market, for freshwater fish[6] was welcome on many a table: in the 1840s the incumbent of Swaffham Bulbeck, Leonard Jenyns – the man who recommended Charles Darwin for the *Beagle* voyage – records the fishermen of his village sending a startling amount of fish from Swaffham Bulbeck Lode, a shallow and narrow waterway, to Cambridge Market each week. Paul and Sally stare out of time at us from a yellowing photograph, for the taking of which they would have had to sit very still.

The Pits started centuries ago with men digging the heavy Kimmeridge clay for the pottery workshops of Babylon, a warren of low buildings across the river from busy Quayside and Waterside and its inns and brewery and docks. (Nobody seems to know why Babylon was called that, but the name was used on old maps.) The work seems to have started about 1200, and the Babylon Ware was fired by peat from the Fen. (More holes in the ground...) By the 1860s there were 80 people in the craft – and then cheaper goods could be brought from far away by the new railway. Until it arrived, potting was the only Ely employment to rival agriculture. And in and out of the Pits, through the narrow cuts and under the railway bridge, there would have been a constant stream of 40 foot lighters, the empty ones going in to be filled with clay dug from the cliff-like working face of the quarry, and coming out low in the water, loaded to their gunwales with the grey stickiness...

For after Vermuyden's draining of the Fens in the 1600s the peat began to dry out, and shrink, and the improved rivers and drains began to be higher and higher above the surrounding fields. The Ouse that in Norman times lazed through many slow channels through the level fen reaching over to Stuntney and Quanea is now many feet above the drained black land. The more successful the draining, the more the fields sank. Clay, lots of it, was needed to proof the banks against leaks: 'puddling and slubbing', they called the horrid sticky business of spreading layers of the stuff on the beds and banks of drained sections of the waterway. Ely's outcropping clay was an ideal source. I know what hard dirty work digging that clay was, for I have quarried it myself...

It's a long story, and starts a while back. Reach Lode and monk-engineered Burwell Lode and Wicken Lode join forces to meet the Cam at the lock at Upware – the name seems to mean 'the upper weir', and any weir of course antedates the introduction in the fourteenth century of the pound lock. (It seems to have been invented in China a couple of centuries earlier.) It was once an important place. The Romans had a sizeable stone warehouse there, built on the tip of the ancient coral reef that rises out of the fen, and probably used it to marshal the produce of the villa estates that ring this rim of the fen. (There was one at Reach.) Then it would be transhipped for the water journey to the garrisons at York and Lincoln, even, some say, to the boundary of the Empire in Germany and the legion at Cologne. In not quite living memory there was once a sizeable wharf on the Cam, and Upware was an important crossing point: a chain ferry, which could take a horse and cart – its slip is still there – took you across to Waterbeach Fen, and was in use well into the 1940s. As with all once busy places, when they stopped being busy things got left behind.

One summer afternoon a friend and I walked there along the river. Someone had been cleaning up: the water plants – phragmites, reed mace, sedges – forming a dense hydrosere in an old dock cut into the bank next to the lock had been cleared out and dumped in heaps on the bank. And there, sunk into the mud, only its stem and stern and gunwales rising above the clear water, was an almost perfectly preserved wooden sailing barge that someone had probably meant to come back for and never did. The rains of winter brimmed it and sank it lower and lower into the welcoming mud. Reeds and sedge grew round where the mast had been stepped.

Now, I knew enough to recognise that this boat was of an unusual type, clearly designed to carry sail, and smaller than the usual fen barge, though the construction method of oak frames and elm planking pegged together with trunnels was the same. So, in some excitement, I

64

got in touch with the National Maritime Museum – after all, excavating boats had become quite fashionable in the decades after the discovery in 1937 of the first Ferriby boat. They took the boat seriously, sent two specialists out to see it, and were happy for me to get a team together to build a coffer dam so that the dock could be drained. A distinguished QC I knew declared the boat in the water to be *res derelicta* – so, finder's keepers, roughly. The local branch of the Inland Waterways Association was enthusiastic, and promised help. Volunteers got in touch. All going, as you might say, swimmingly…

But. The man on whose land the dock abutted, with no malice afterthought – after all, he was interested in building a small marina, as we found later, and nobody had thought to tell him of the potential importance of the boat – cleaned the dock out with a dragline. All that was left when he had finished, as we could see on the next visit, was a lot of broken wood: the massive oak knees, cut for strength from where the tree branched so that the grain followed the curve of the knee, were all scattered, the elm planking was matchwood.

Yet we had a head of steam… a lot of people had become interested, and at a meeting it was realised that the wooden boats – very like those on the Stour which Constable painted – of the barge traffic of the fens had hardly been documented, and had now been completely superseded first by strings of low-maintenance steel lighters and in the end by trains and lorries. Those wooden lighters, from at least the mid eighteenth century, provided the heavy transport for a large swathe of England, reaching far beyond the Fenland or the Ouse-Nene complex of waterways. I have a photo, taken about

1900, of a gang of them moored at a then treeless Reach Hythe, waiting for cargo. Without them, the produce of the newly drained fens, essential to the feeding of the growing industrial towns, simply could not have been moved in sufficient quantities, especially when roads were foul in winter. They were often operated in gangs of half-a-dozen or so, linked stem to stern, and a couple of men could manage a string. It did not really matter how slowly they went – and they did go slowly, no faster than a horse could pull or a fair wind push, until the steam tugs came and imperiously allowed no dawdling. What mattered was they were moving tons of stuff reliably, as no horse and cart could do.

Then someone said that it might be worth looking in Roswell Pits to see what obsolete things had been sunk there. The River Board indulgently said we could look… and so came the day when Peter Heward in his little cabin cruiser slowly cruised up and down the pits, with two men in snorkels and flippers towed behind. Nothing… and then, just as we were resigned to having drawn blank, three wooden 40 foot lighters at once, sunk by the side of a small scrub-covered island. Two were far gone, and had probably been there for many, many decades. The third seemed in excellent condition. We were in business.

How do you build a coffer dam even in water only five or so feet deep? None of us had done it before. The theory was all right… sacks full of clay laid like huge bricks… I begged hundreds of plastic fertiliser sacks from a farmer who seemed unaccountably (but for us fortunately) to have a shed full of them. The River Board were again indulgent: yes, we could quarry the clay, yes, we could ferry it across to the island by poling, like some outsize punt, a 40 foot steel lighter that was minding its own business doing nothing. (It needed baling out.) And so we began the long, long job of filling the sacks, Peter's boat getting filthier and filthier with these muddy men scrambling in and out of it.

It was a long job, indeed. Weekend after weekend stretched into June, then July, then August. I bought a cheap plastic inflatable from one of the snorkelers so I could get across to the island on my own, and spent many hours with a mattock digging at the tough laminations of the clay and shovelling it into bags. It was impossible, as my shoulders and back got more and more tired, not to pity the men who year in year out did for a living what I was doing – well, if not for fun on my part, at least with no compulsion. 'Gaulters' they were called, and they cut at the face of the clay, shovelled it into heavy wooden barrows with iron-shod wheels, and ran the load along narrow slippery planks to tip it stickily into the waiting lighter. (And then it had to be dug out again where it was to be used. Tough work in all weathers. And no chance of a hot shower at the end of the day.) I had looked things up about the clay, too: and knew, with a certain awe, that I was standing in/on the bed of a shallow sea where 150 million years ago silt and mud settled on the sea floor, particle by particle burying hosts of dead things.

During a break to ease my back... easy to fall in the warm sun into a sort of daydream... Imagine... Or remember, perhaps.

And before you know where you are, the daydream begins to slide into a dream...

...the bottom of the sea. The water is warm, very warm, but you have no standard of comparison to know that. Creatures fly past: a myriad little ones with tentacles trailing behind their whorled shell – but the older ones can get huge if they find enough prey. The fluted stems of sea lilies rise from the ooze, their tentacles waving to catch the creatures who are meat and drink to them. The ancestors of oysters open their shelly valves to filter the tiny creatures from the water: their lips have sensors that smell and taste their food. And you cannot see far, for over all is a mist, a rain, of particles, slowly, ever so slowly, building up the level of the ooze. There is time, lots of it... One day unimaginable creatures, who walk on two legs and use tools, will call what you lie on the Kimmeridge Beds. This period has got some six million years, and the next one will last even longer, till from deep space an asteroid intrudes and changes the world for ever.

But the world does change, even slowly, without asteroids. The currents of the sea swirl and alter as Gaia shrugs, and on the clay you have patiently watched being made, they lay down sand, sand, sand, greenish because it has a lot in it of what will one day be called glauconite. Then she stirs again, and now the water is full of the limey exoskeletons of dead creatures, diatoms, whose cycle of life is over, and the rain of what will be chalk and clunch is unceasing, for these waters are fertile, rich in food. One day you will be food too, and your atoms be cast back into the melt from which things unimaginable will rise. Until the sun who makes these currents and from whose forge every particle once came, dies.

A fly – one of the big black ones – settled on my nose. To work. The clay was full of the grey fossils of that dead world: those tiny ammonites as common as blackberries, crinoid 'lilies' – though they look like plants, they are carnivores, related to the starfish and the sea urchins – bivalves like modern clams, *gryphaea*. Occasionally my mattock would split open a harder lump to reveal a vug, a void formed in the matrix and lined with the glittering spikes of dog tooth spar – calcite. I have a cabinet of these things which I happily show to anyone interested and to many who are not but are too polite to say so. Though distracted by what I found, I did fill sacks, the plastic slippery with slimy clay, and once did manage the huge 'punt' on my own across the hundred yards of water to the site. It builds up quite some momentum even with only one man punting and I did not confess to the others when they came that it was my ramming it that had demolished the beginnings of one side of the dam.

The dam got built: hundreds of sacks laid by men in wetsuits standing in the water, the rest of us passing them out of the lighter to them. The next worry was whether it would hold when we emptied it. But how are we to empty it?

Ask and it shall be given unto you... we appealed to Cambridge University Officer Training Corps, thinking they might know where we could borrow a high-volume pump, and sure enough, the Territorials happily delivered one to Waterside at Ely one fine Sunday morning in late summer. But Waterside is a long way from the Pits...we hadn't thought of that... an urgent appeal to Appleyard Lincoln's boatyard across the river secured the loan of a pontoon. As Peter's boat drew it out of the little dock, a kingfisher flashed past us, hurrying to another perch along the river. (Do you still see his/her descendants on in the middle of the town on Waterside nowadays?)

The dam held: just. We pumped out the boat. And then, an ominous bulge appeared in the bottom of the line of sacks, slowly swelling, until the wall suddenly collapsed. The water rushed in. But. As it rose round the boat she seemed to shudder, as if shaking off long slumber. To our surprise, and delight, she was beginning to float – low in the water to be sure, but undoubtedly afloat, after probably the best part of a century. And she was sound enough, with pumping, to be towed up to Cambridge by the river she had known of old, before the coming of the railways killed the teeming water traffic of these parts. Her first home was the Museum of Technology. Then, dried out, and stabilised, her elm and oak found a home with the Fenland Lighter Project at Peterborough.

But all that was then... Now is now, even if subtly nuanced by the chiaroscuro the memory of 'Then' casts on it. We have come to love the river in the still mornings when the sun is just up, and the early mist lies shallow on the water, and the flats are veiled, with only the Tower and Octagon of Ely Cathedral catching the golden light. A duck's '*quack*, quack, quack' out of the mist stresses the quietness. The dog's muzzle is wet with the dew on the grass, and he sneezes. The clock strikes. Or there are those evenings, especially as the year ages – time it well, when most people are eating or already doing whatever it is they do in the evenings – and the place is deserted, and the only sound is the alarm of a moorhen as Milo gets too close, or the 'chack' of a coot. We don't talk. The sky to the east is grading into its evening violet, but the west is still bright, and the Tower and Octagon stand out sharp and dark against the sunset. Looking from this deserted bank by the quiet flowing Ouse, that view cannot have changed since the monks would have been gathering for Vespers at this hour.

We walk slowly up the lane from the river to the railway crossing. In the ditch a magnificent stand of the strange Equisetum, at half a metre taller than I have ever seen before, reaches up to the light. It is a plant that first appears in the early Jurassic: I have found its fossils high on a moraine in Spitsbergen, plants that knew a world far warmer than this and grew when Spitsbergen was on the Equator. (Even rocks do not stay put in one place, let alone people.) Its giant relatives, some 38 metres tall, fell in course of time into the fenny mould that made the Coal Measures. I remember the thrill, not all that many years ago, when my unskilled hammer split a lump of rock to reveal the print of the green softness that had bent to the warm wind of an equatorial climate. My mind plays round the thought of these (today puny) plants growing in the Kimmeridge clay their huge ancient ancestors would have known. One of the oldest plants on earth, here at our feet... the dinosaurs – the ones that were herbivorous – might have grazed on the foliage. It grew in Lancashire too, but not tall like this: as children we used to play with its hard abrasive stems, pulling them apart at the socket-like nodes. Even then, I thought it looked – well, not as a plant *should* look.

And I find, in William Harrisons' *Description of England* (1577), that it is with 'horsetail' that 'Fletchers and Combemakers doe rubbe and polish their worke.'

The River

You will have realised that I find it hard to ignore the past: it's like hearing a ground running below a musical harmony, deepening and colouring the present. That – shall we say double vision? – has become much more pronounced as I have grown older. Equisetum reminds of woodlands no man ever saw, whose coal stored the sunlight and heat that man released in homely fire and blast furnace and steam engine. Peel back the layers, see the moment for what it is, just the top layer and not the last. The ancient woods – well, not ancient by equisetum standards – of these lands, when you could have walked from Ireland to Russia and beyond, their ghosts are still there too: and a table in a Cathedral recalls them. Then, water: the water that made this land, in sediments long ago, and in the shaping by river and flood and sea. Here, if anywhere, you cannot ignore the dykes against the sea, and the work of men's hands in the draining of the land – one of the marvels of the world, I think it. But like fire, you can use water, but you cannot tame it. One day it will win.

On the whole, the Cam and the Ouse it joins have been taught to behave themselves. But I once knew and dearly loved a man who as a small child in 1920 had been taken from Cambridge in a horse-drawn chaise by his parents to see an exceptionally high tide at Waterbeach. This was of course long before the present Denver Sluice was built. He saw a tiny tidal bore – he told me it was about two inches high – sweep past. For the Cam is naturally tidal that far upstream. So far, only that far.

In Cambridge it is so easy to forget the imperatives of water in this part of the world, the area of England with the lowest rainfall yet where the battle with water has gone on for centuries. It is much harder to forget the water in Ely, where every approach is across a drained lakebed. Travel by water was normal. Follow on foot or in canoe the little river from Reach, which is fed at the spring line where the 'high land' (as they used to call it) slopes into the fen, and you are soon high above the fields for the three miles to Upware where Reach Lode joins the Cam. Then comes the long, long reach to Ely, and at no point are you not aware of – you cannot even see – the rich drained land below you, and how vulnerable it is. I remember sharply realising that vulnerability when I did that journey for the first time. When we moved to Reach we soon encountered people – like Albert and Seth and Reuben, our neighbours – who could remember winters when the astonished cattle in the fen were enisled on

74

the patches of higher ground, even one awful February when the fire in the kitchen had to be made on a layer of bricks to get the hearth above the level of the water in the room. The snow lying late in Bedfordshire, then a sudden warming and a lot of wind and rain from the west, and the pumps could not cope. Getting across the flooded land – well, men used stilts – 'fen camels' – (which also helped you see over the tall reeds, phragmites, which can grow to over 6 feet) and the spring frogs were so numerous I am told some called them 'fen nightingales', or (further north) 'Lincolnshire bagpipes'.[7]

Albert remembered the time the banks burst where the river ran its course way above the level of the fields, and every man and boy for miles around was drafted to the breach to fill sandbags to stanch the flow, while a lighter full of gault clay dug from Roswell Pits was held against the bank to lessen the force of the great cascade. That does not happen now, thanks to the Cut Off Channel, which runs round the Fens to catch the water off the higher land and take it directly to Denver. (That was part of Vermuyden's brilliant seventeenth century original design, but nobody dug it until the 1960s.) You can still get a glimpse of what the Fens were like in winter when you drive from Ely to Welney over the Washes between the Bedford Rivers, where water that cannot be let out of Denver Sluice because of the tide is held until the ebb starts. Water stretches as far as the eye can see, the willows on the banks seem to enjoy paddling in it, and for hosts of duck and geese and swans this is heaven-sent. But not too good for people in the old days. Dickens' picture of the Lincolnshire fen floods in *Bleak House*, or Dorothy Sayers' superb evocation of floods in a fen village in *The Nine Tailors*… Dorothy Sayers knew this part of the country well: she grew up in Bluntisham as the daughter of the vicar (a Lawrentian title of delicious inappropriateness!), and her fictional flooded village has a church which is an amalgam of St Peter's in Upwell, Terrington St Clement and Walpole St Peter near Lynn. People sheltering in the one building likely to be on higher ground above the water when the floods were out was all too common.

And thinking (were we?) about the volume of trade the rivers once carried… It's obvious that water was/is the easiest and cheapest way to move really heavy, bulky stuff, and right up to the coming of the railways, water transport dominated. The roads the Romans had left were still there in the Middle Ages, but with little or no maintenance over the centuries had deteriorated to quagmires in winter and potholed tracks in summer. Wheeled traffic was painful – literally, with all those bumps. After about 1400, carriages for the very wealthy might have a sort of suspension of the body on chains, but with their swaying these were hardly comfortable – the French called them *chars branlants*. There were no springs until the 1770s or so. Travel by cart was painfully slow, and if you could go faster on horseback you were still very much exposed to weather and hazards. So everywhere you look there is evidence of the importance of rivers, and if you haven't got a river, well, make one: some of my ancestors did well in the canal boom, until the speed of the railway killed the demand for the narrowboats they built on the Staffordshire Knot, and they had to become farm labourers and miners.

The Ouse and Cam, even before fen drainage and straightening, were important. The Ouse is after all the fourth biggest river in England, 143 miles long, and before it was emasculated by the new Bedford Rivers at Earith it was a force to be reckoned with when in spate. The Romans used the rivers to get goods to the sea; there was probably never a time when they were not carrying traffic. Canute was on his way to Ely for the Candlemas Feast in February one year, and, the full stream being against the rowers, progress was very slow. The chronicler tells us at that the king was impatient, and as soon as they neared the Isle, 'the king rose up in the middle of his men and directed the boatmen to make for the little port at full speed [hence Littleport]', where he got horses. Even much later, water travel was a serious option: Edmund Carter's *History of the County of Cambridge* (1753) reports that 'for the conveniency of passengers, and heavy goods to and from Cambridge' a boat left Ely every Tuesday and Friday for Cambridge; the 20-mile journey took six hours.

Later still, lighters towed by a horse, or under a sail pushed by a north wind, would carry heavy stuff up to the foundries and gas works at Cambridge, and the river would see little steam tugs like the old *Nellie* or *Olga* with their tall smokestacks pulling many a string of lighters. Only a century ago… Even then, the high days of inland navigation had already declined a lot after the railway line was extended from Cambridge in the 1840s, and then extended further to Lynn and Norwich. (There was even a little line of just a few miles through Grunty Fen from Ely to Sutton.) Yet even as late as the 1860s there is a record of 'half a hundred black barges' that went downstream to Lynn and came upstream to Cambridge 'laden with coal or heaped high with turf and sedge'.*

I once knew a lot about the last days of that trade and its crafts. I remember reading about (for example) the legendary horse called Captain, around 1900, who pulled barges and would unbidden leap the ditches and fences as he came to them, knowing to let the barges catch him up a bit to give him slack in the very long tow rope... (A short rope simply pulled the boat into the bank.) The pubs along the water remember that time, but now cater for a quite different sort of clientèle. In them the bargees could get drink and a bed, and oats for the horse that drew the barge, and a warm out of the wind – for working the boats was a tough life. No wonder you learned to swear. The Cutter at Ely by the wharves; the Fish and Duck, where once there was a ferry so you could get over from the other bank; then, at Upware, just by where the chain ferry (in its last iteration) used to cross, there was from the 1780s the Black Swan, which after Trafalgar was renamed the Lord Nelson. Its gable end had painted on it, in huge letters, a reassurance to the passing barges: 'Five Miles from Anywhere. No Hurry.' Then came three winding miles to Bottisham Lock, where the Conservators of the Cam take over the management of the river under the provisions of the Act of 1703. Then came The Sluice at Clayhithe (now called The Bridge), and busy Horningsea, which once was full of pubs and still has two good ones. And then Fen Ditton

---

* J. W. Clark in T.D. Atkinson, *Cambridge Described*, p. xxv; T. R. Glover, *Cambridge Retrospect*, 5

and its Plough, with its garden reaching down to the river. Now the only passing boats are pleasure craft and racing shells. Then, as the barge entered Cambridge, the chimney of the gasworks and the foundry in Thompson's Lane would be prominent on the skyline as the boats passed the beloved Pike and Eel – that is gone now, a victim given to greed and the profit of expensive houses – and the sixteenth century Fort St George, and then the George and Dragon, once the last pub on the right bank before the wharves on Quayside.

Busy indeed. Almost every house and field from Horningsea to Cambridge has its dock nibbling into the bank. Now they shelter pleasure craft, or the secrecy of reeds and osiers and coot and heron. The Romans had docks there, too, to serve the pottery which made a black ware found all over East Anglia. Horningsea – its name gives it away, 'Horning's Island' (and Horning may be someone's nickname, 'bastard': I do like that. What is the story?): here the water, which for the last few miles when you do this walk has been getting less and less above the fields almost without one's noticing, is lower than the land for the first time.

Footsore long before the end, I once followed that towpath all one early spring day, one Holy Week, to Cambridge... I set off through the extremely low underpass under the railway where almost every week some van would take its roof off, then a right turn onto a long trudge along the high flood bank. It was quite early. The noise from hurrying commuting traffic on the new bypass could be heard for a mile or so. Here the path ran high above the black fields over towards the bluff of Stuntney. Swans dotted the fields. Some fields shone in the light where sheets of plastic cover them, and the wind occasionally got under the sheets so that there seemed to be waves scudding to the horizon on small lakes. Once they would have been real flashes, when the winter river ran high and all its braided channels would have been full. One of those channels must have run close to the bluff on the top of which the Cathedral stands, for the twelfth century *Liber Eliensis* tells how Canute and his queen, Emma[8] of Normandy, travelling by boat to Ely for Candlemas, heard the monks singing in the Abbey church – it wasn't a Cathedral till 1109. The chronicler then says 'to express his joy, he composed this song in English:

> *Merie sungen þe muneches binnen Ely*
> *þa Cnut cyng reu þer by.*
> *Roweð cnites noer the lant*
> *and here we þes muneches sæng.'*

> *(Merrily sang the monks in Ely,*
> *When Cnut the king rowed by.*
> *'Row, men, nearer the land,*
> *And let us hear these monks sing.)*

It's good to know that the choir of Ely was as worth hearing then as the Cathedral choir is now.

Canute and Emma must have had an open February. On another February, again going to Ely for Candlemas, the fens were frozen hard, but the king got there with the help of a 'large and rugged man from the Isle, Brihtmær surnamed Budde on account of his bulk.' Brihtmær (who won his freedom by this act) led them across the ice from

80

Soham to Ely with the king following in a wagon, and 'everybody marvelled that he should have attempted such a great act of daring.' Along the route of the old timber causeway across the marsh, the shortest crossing from the high bluff of Stuntney, Stunta's Island, to Ely, the traffic from Soham thunders, the note changing as it drops from the high land to cross the peat, just as you can tell from miles away when the King's Lynn to Cambridge train's track runs on peat or on clay.

Once again, as always, place names intrigue me. I do wonder who Stunta was, and why he was called by a name that means 'foolish.' Idle thoughts of an idle fellow... but the real people behind the placenames do matter, even if their stories are now unknowable to us.

After a few miles I came to Pope's Corner, where the Old West River and the Cam meet. The name has nothing to do with the lost pre-Reformation world. In 1850 a man called Richard Pope built a pub here. The Fish and Duck was big: seven rooms and 12 stable blocks, all to cater for the trade on the river, much of which was horse-drawn. I remember a decent Burwell brick building, with no frills, just the good sense and proportion that the Georgian pattern books then still in use taught builders. (And a decent pint of beer. We sometimes of a summer evening would make our way down there from Upware in the Zodiac dinghy.) Now, no pub – the house was demolished a good time ago – just a sprawling marina offering everything from basic chandlery and Calor gas to electricity hook-up and Elsan disposal. Pleasure boats all...

As I walked along I kept coming across little afloat communities, in all sorts and conditions of boats. Some boats were/are little better than soap dishes with pretensions – hardly boats at all. There are others that in this their old age remember the North Sea and the shallow coasts of Holland – the bluff bows and the lee boards are the giveaway. But they will never go to the old grey widowmaker again. A surprising number are of that lineage, reminding of the entwined history over millennia of the windy flat shores of Holland and Frisia and this part of the world. They are so much more commodious than the narrowboats – like the one on which my old pupil, friend and colleague Simone lived with her husband. Some of these boats, moored on the washes well away from Cambridge, where the river spreads itself in a wet winter and the cattle graze in summer to the protest of plovers and the grousing of geese, have been there long enough to have gardens. Hens churckle and scratch round feeders.

Birds: duck, of course, but all the way up to Horningsea the river seemed to be full of great crested grebes. I love them, and their elaborate surprised-looking heads that seem to be wearing a prick-eared helmet of feathers. I do wonder, though, what evolutionary advantage it gives them when they are chasing their prey underwater. Unlike shape and colouration, it seems to have nothing to do with display or sexual dimorphism, as with almost all other species, and it seems almost impossible to tell the sexes apart. (Over my lifetime, that has got to be much more of a problem, not just with grebes.) The grebes can, one hopes: and I find a certain magic in seeing their strange courting ritual when each, breast to breast, presents the other with a scrap of weed. She/he is cheap to keep... 'would my beloved like some weed?' ('No, not *that* sort of weed...') There was a nest in the reeds by the Fish and Duck. I caught a glimpse of it, and either Mummy or

Daddy was on it with either Mummy or Daddy patrolling the river – both sexes incubate, making things yet more complicated. The world is charged with wonder, with the glory of God. Everywhere is a theophany. It shines through even for a wandering mind like mine.

The path took me through the new nature reserve, an example of our belated attempt to atone for the harm we have done to our world and our fellow creatures. Highland cows munched at me, thoughtfully. (Highland??? They could hardly get lower, for bits of their pasture are below sea level.) Then a big surprise: a water buffalo munching the weed that carpeted the water in a dyke. He was a long way from his ancestral home. I came along the droveway to the Five Miles from Anywhere at Upware, (No Hurry), promising myself, and Left Hip (who was mithering), a rest and a marmalade sandwich when I got beyond it – and I have to go beyond and get upwind, for some clot was burning a heap of plastic fertiliser sacks and the smell and smoke was awful, choking.

It's a strange place, this hamlet I know so well. It's clearly shrunk from what it once was, but I doubt it was ever that big. It's at the end of the straight lode, which some say the Romans were the first to dig, the head of which is virtually in the garden of my old house at Reach. They had here a substantial barn or store, with stone foundations, behind where the Victorian old school building stands. Upware was one of the last places in the Fens where the men grew their hair long, and walked up the Lode each year at Rogationtide to the annual Reach Fair to get it cut and to enjoy their annual punch-up with the men of Reach. Once, in the 1860s and 70s, the pub was home to the Upware Republic, a disreputable society of indolent and muscular Cambridge undergraduates who sculled down river for binges of drinking, fighting, fishing, shooting and, in a good winter, the grace of skating. A certain Richard Fielder, a MA of Jesus College, took up residence at the inn, and called himself King of Upware and dominated the Republic and the countryside around with his fists and his scathing tongue. He would fight anyone, bargee or gentleman, at any time, usually winning, and pitching them into the river. He had a special vessel he called a gotch, which held two quarts of beer. He was of good family and high ability, but incurably lazy. His family gave him an allowance to live on, payable provided that he kept away. He it was who originally painted 'Five Miles from Anywhere: No Hurry' on the gable of the inn where he lounged, smoked, drank and fought with the watermen. In the end, apparently, as undergraduates became more serious-minded after University reforms, he retired to Folkestone where he lived in some degree of comfort and respectability.

I thought of him as I walked over the lock at the end of Reach Lode – if you know something of the history of a place, it won't go away, that presentness of the past, always insistent. In fact, the older I get the nearer the past seems. And I wondered what really drove him, what lay behind the longhaired, filthy, violent caricature he made of himself. Despair? What the mediaevals would have called *accidia*, sloth – which is not mere laziness, but something far more deadly – and we might call depression? It's a subtle trap, always ready to spring, and damned hard to get out of. It can take many forms: not least keeping yourself so busy, your mind so noisy, that you can hide from yourself, deflecting the still, small voice into an ever-deferred future. Which is why a long solitary walk can be a risk: you don't know what that slow rhythm and silence might let surface.

The Washes at Upware, where the Cam in flood can spread itself wide between the flood banks while the sluice at Denver waits for the tide to turn so the water can drain into the receding sea, only a few weeks before had been full of water. They had been loud at nightfall with the calls of duck and geese; now they were drying fast. I hear redshank, but can't see them. How they can feed when the usually soft ground was so hard beat me. A few plovers did their aerial ballet as if only for me – not so, of course. There used to be many, many more. There were greylags, alert and graceful, and the vulgar and excitable Canadas. Then I heard the first cuckoo that spring. Delius? (Letter to *The Times*? – but no, that was when it was a civilised paper.) Yes, definitely, at this spot and with that thought, time for a rest.

Rest? Some hopes. I had just started my sandwich when I felt something pull on my trouser leg. A mallard. 'How wonderful,' I thought for an instant, 'perhaps the fear of Man is gone.' For I long for the barrier of fear between the species to break down. As it can do, for example, in those curious reciprocal loves with our animals, where two remote worlds of sense and perception meet and touch, as it did with my dear Hector the Labrador or my daughter's pony Robbie. But no, of course. That is not yet. This was an importunate bandit of a drake who had clearly realised that humans could be a source of easy food. He climbed onto my legs, and, one orange foot on each, marched straight up to my chest and made a grab for the sandwich. He broke a substantial chunk off, but it dropped into my crotch, whereupon down went his head, and in a moment was happily gobbling it. A curious sensation, not wholly unpleasant...

Stuffing what was left of the sandwich into my mouth – spilling more crumbs – I raised the camera, and as I did so he made a grab for it, perhaps 'thinking' it a new and interesting sort of sandwich that humans should not keep to themselves. Hence a very foreshortened photo of a duck. But what goes on in a duck's head? Probably a lot more, and in a different way, than our reductive mindset allows.

He was not impressed, tidied up the crumbs, walked all round me to make sure there was nothing else edible, and then waddled off to have a nice refreshing sleep. Some animals are indeed bandits. There was a time on the hills above Buxton, when, having opened the car door while I ate my lunch, a wet sheep tried to get onto my lap and nick my sandwich. I gave it a Rolo – which kept it quiet for quite a time, enough for me to finish lunch. Which was sandwiches made from Sunday's roast lamb.

My left hip complained as I got up, and told my right heel to back him up. I told them both to shut up. I passed the duck decoy on the wash just upstream from Upware – just by where a century ago there was a little hamlet. The place is almost deserted now: just one farm. There was a chapel, built by public subscription, people sending tiny amounts of money from far away, some – emigrants from this area? – even from the USA. There used to be a post office, still operative but with little trade when we came to this part of the world, which old Mrs Stanford ran. Her husband ran a sort of taxi service – when he was not busy. The decoy is now fenced securely with chainlink and barbed wire and notices saying 'private'. It is odd to think that what was one of the many places where duck were taken in their winter thousands for the tables of Cambridge and London is now a sanctuary for them, and for the muddy unloveliness of carp. In the thicket of small willows and osier and hawthorn, the cuckoo calls again. You get plenty of reminders of vicissitude and the ephemerality of things on this sort of walk. Yet do we humans actually want permanence, stability? We say we do, but we do go odd ways to get it.

Then the going got poor, really uncomfortable. For a couple of miles cattle had grazed the bank while the winter mud was deep and doughy, and now this long drought had hardened the hoofprints into sharp, ankle-twisting concrete. Left Hip has something to say about it... 'You just try it... this is no place for a respectable hip...I deserve better. Why did you bring me here? No consideration.'

The later afternoon became unpleasantly muggy. I had not brought enough water with me, and collapsed onto a bench in the garden of the Fort St George pub with a thirst – well, Lent and all that, and I was supposed to be off alcohol, so no pint... but a pint of shandy was surely venial? It was very, very welcome. I thought of nothing, just sat, with my feet up on the opposite bench. I began to muse about the journey... walking away from Etheldreda's island, through a landscape, which more than any other in what is now called England, has been made in the last 300 years – those three centuries which have seen the abolition of the spiritual in the orthodox, materialist Western mindset. Sometimes it is good to go against the stream.

There is a busy railway bridge over the river, and the path goes under it to take you to the water meadows and the places where Milo and his friends love to run and swim. The trains – the long freight ones especially, which I suppose have taken the place of the strings of lighters – rumble deafeningly across the water only a very few feet above your head as you walk through and you can see their undercarriage through the gaps between the girders. Yet untroubled pigeons nest on those girders, inches from the wheels. The smooth water slicks by the cutwaters with no sound I can hear. Where the divided streams rejoin there is a little standing wave, a smooth muscle waiting to be flexed. Don't ignore rivers, and what is in them.

Just by the bridge the city fathers have designated a carpark as the Fishermen's Car Park. They kindly recognise that modern coarse fishing, even for the mainly inedible denizens of the slow rivers of this part of the world, needs trolleys, tents, seats, boxes of complex equipment, rod rests, bite detectors, sometimes a stove or instant barbecue, a case of beer. It's all a far cry from a very young me, catching the lively perch of Leg o' Mutton Pool, on holiday in Talke, in Staffordshire, the village where my father grew up and which he had not been able to get out of quick enough. (They told me that once upon a time the men used to bathe in that pool when, black with coal, they came up from the pits.) I had a primitive rod no child now would be seen dead with, a little wooden star back reel, cotton line, a treasured porcupine quill float. Bait was worms dug from my uncle's garden. Rod rest was a forked twig set in the ground.

But the men by the river with their copious armoury seem happy enough, as I was. So they do also at their

88

quiet fishing matches along the bank of Reach Lode at Upware. Evenly spaced they sit, dreamily watching the water. Not many want to talk as you pass. But occasionally they can be persuaded to become eloquent about the monsters that lurk in the dark below and among the gently waving weeds, how a big pike will rise and gulp down a duckling – indeed, I myself have seen adorable moorhen chicks, little balls of black fluff that can almost run along the top of the water, disappear in a quiet swirl. A water bailiff on the upper Cam told me once that by the mill at Grantchester he had seen a pike take a happily swimming Jack Russell terrier, and he had had to calm its hysterical owner down. Pike can indeed get big. But years ago someone introduced the predatory zander, now a challenging, sought after fish, hard to fool into being caught, and they have made themselves at home. Seen head on, with open mouth, even a small one can look fearsome: I would not like to be a roach.

My old friend Mike Greenhill can turn his hand to most things, and is a mighty fisherman and fine shot. I have seen him grow up from cheerful, mischievous lad, as talkative as the tame jackdaw who perched on his shoulder or head, to grizzled and roguish middle age. He has caught many zander, and tells me they are excellent eating. (They are: once in Vienna I had a fillet with chips. The fish is native to eastern Europe.) But there are other creatures down there…

Carp can run to a big size – over 60lb indeed, and are, they tell me, bonny fighters. (I think they are tasteless too, but let that pass.) But the real secret monster is the catfish, which can reach over 100lb and be as long as a man is tall without achieving beauty. (They are one of the few fish that can also breathe air.) I have eaten them in Hungary, where they can grow to a great size in rivers so large they make the Ouse look like a dribble. In Szeged I was shown a photo of one catfish so big a man was able to put his head in its open mouth. (Nobody mentioned why he wanted to.) Indeed, in that country catfish are a delicacy: they say that the only bits you can't eat are the gills. A few have been released into the rivers of East Anglia, illegally. Mike told me of one night at Upware when he caught one: it took him an hour and more to get it to the bank, and his arms were aching before he tried to lift the monster. He never managed to weigh it: but it was, he said, about six feet long. It had been caught before: there was a scar under its jaw, and a very distinctive healed wound on its head. The beast, tired (as was Mike) after its battle, swam off into the dark and Mike packed up his gear and went home as dawn was breaking.

Not the end of the story… next year, fishing not the Great Ouse but the Lark, again at night, he felt a massive take and struck hard. The hook held, and the hours-long battle began. Mike banked the fish eventually, and drew its exhausted bulk onto the flattened reeds, and lit a roll-up. But then his headtorch lit up a scar he recognised… 30 miles that fish had travelled, only to come up against Mike again. As he told me this story – which he does well – Mike said, with that grin I know of old, 'Do you know, mate, that fish had a look in his eye that showed he was thinking, "O bugger me, not you again!"'

It does make one wonder about letting Milo swim.

Eel Island

Some say the name of Ely derives from 'Eel Island', and in the Middle Ages rents and dues were indeed often paid in eels: in 1086 the small town of Chatteris paid the Abbot of Ely a due of 1,500 eels and the village of Doddington paid the huge number of 27,150. (Why that huge difference? I must find out one day.) Stuntney, just a mile away across the fen, was worth 24,000 eels, Littleport 17,000. They would be taken in nets, in grigs, or with eel glaives (now illegal) thrust into the mud where the fish like to bury themselves. Many men earned their living as fishermen. The abbey needed those eels, for there was no usable building stone for the abbey nearby and they had to buy it from the Abbey at Peterborough, which claimed rights in the quarries at Barnack: 8,000 eels a year it cost them.[9] But they still had plenty… and the number of fast days in mediaeval Christendom when meat was off limits meant that everyone ate a lot of fish.

And not only people. One lazy afternoon we were sitting by the river near the Cutter Inn, idly watching the river go by. As one too rarely does... A cormorant was fishing, but each time it surfaced its dive seemed to have been fruitless. It was floating lower and lower in the water as its feathers got wetter, and soon on an empty crop it would have to go and dry its wings. Then, success! It emerged with a youngish eel in its long, sharply hooked beak, a vigorous and fit young eel, which was not pleased. The cormorant was not going to let go, not after all that trouble, despite the eel's wrapping itself lithely round its captor's neck, and writhing so quickly you could hardly see its movements. (How I remember that writhing when as lads fishing off Rossall Beach at home we caught the migrating eels we did not want and had to get them off the hook!) The difficulty was that to swallow the eel the bird had to change its grip from the middle of the eel and get it head first: a tough job.

After a few minutes a small crowd had gathered, some vociferously taking the part of the eel, some of the bird. Some dogs were just bored to be made to stay in one place: others strained at their leashes in eagerness to join in the fray. It must have been a good twenty minutes before the bird did manage to get the eel, still flailing, in the right position to be swallowed. Its tail slowly disappeared, still bravely waving, and you could easily see from the peristaltic bulges in the skin of the bird's neck that the rest of the eel was still putting up a fight even as it made its way down the bird's dark gullet to its crop. As the last of the flicking tail disappeared, a small cheer rose. I once, on my own on a lonely shore in Arran, saw a similar long struggle between a heron fishing in the shallows and a small plaice. It had it, as it were, broadside on: and there was no way it could swallow that size of fish except head first. It took a very long time, and once it nearly dropped it. Predators don't always have it all their own way.

Every so often the drains and lodes need dredging, and in winter and spring the dragline would crawl its slow way along the waterside, and swing round like some great beast from its gulp in the water to disgorge loads of grey mud on the land behind it. There was a time when that mud would be full of squirming eels, and I can remember people in the village forty or so years ago going out with buckets to pick them up after the Lode had been dredged. For they are excellent meaty food, solid flesh that goes extremely well fried in collops with butter and parsley – and for that matter many other ways. I did myself go out with my own bucket, even made my own eel grig out of wire mesh and had it in the river at the bottom of the garden baited with rotten meat – it did not catch anything, alas. To my credit I did try to put any of the little eels I found in the mud back in water as quickly as I could so that they did not dry out, and so would survive and grow up big and strong. It is difficult not to feel admiration for them – and they are delicious as well. Everyone knows how the mature eels migrate to breed in the Sargasso Sea from all over the eastern USA and Western Europe, the males swimming at one level and the females at another, as if not speaking to each other until they get down, shall we say, to business. They can reach immense ages: 85 has been recorded. The little elvers take about three years to get back to the rivers their parents left. I have myself seen on the Wyre in Lancashire an elver run, the little creatures nearly transparent (hence the name 'glass eels') and so close together you wondered there was room for water. But not nowadays...

One night – it would have been May or June, I think, only a handful of years ago – I was out down Reach Poor's Fen with the dog for his last sniff, widdle and squat before bed. I was much later than usual – I had a paper I was writing on Chaucer to finish – and it was the dark of the moon. Even so, I took him a long way down the Fen, for there was just enough light to see, I needed a proper leg stretch, and after all I knew the paths along the droves like the back of my hand. Then, coming toward me, I saw headlights. Given that we had had a certain amount of poaching of the roe deer by oafs who have no idea about the dangers of using a rifle from a car in a flat landscape – or do not care – and who have been known to leave a wounded animal to die, my hackles bristled. I called the dog to heel in case there was trouble: it would not have been the first time.

The lights came nearer – a big van – and I stepped to one side, out of his way, hoping to get a sight of his number plate as he passed me. But he stopped right by me. Down came the window as he turned the engine off. Trouble? The dog growled quietly.

'Bet you are wondering what I am doing here at this time of night?'

'Well, yes, actually, I was.'

'Well, don't worry. I am an eel-catcher and I am the last one, I think, in the Fens who makes his living that way.'

This was a different story indeed.

'My traps are in the Lode. I only come down here at night because those damned *didakois** will steal them – and my fish – if they know where I set them. Can't trust anybody...' We must have talked for a good half hour about eels, about how many we lads use to catch off the beach at Rossall when we were fishing for the Autumn codling. The dog was bored. We always cursed those eels, because so often they greedily swallowed the bait and hook whole, and covered your gear with slime, and wrapped their lithe bodies all round your hand and arm as you tried to unhook them. I recalled that story Arthur Ransome tells in one of his books of the eel catcher in the Broads and his eel babs of worms, which he drew up onto his boat in the middle of the night with a Medusa's head of eels wriggling from it, refusing to let go their bite. When he wrote *Coot Club* in 1934 that plethora was perfectly usual. But, the man – his name was Peter – said, 'There are hardly any now', and he had a hard job making a living. What was once cheap food – and good food too – is now a delicacy, and the price has reflected that.

It turned out to be an extremely friendly encounter, though one tinged with sadness, frustration and anger at the rape of our planet by big business and the thoughtlessness of fools who can't see beyond their own noses and don't care if they can. For eels, those nuisances that only a few decades ago we anglers tried not to catch, are now listed as critically endangered on the International Union for Conservation of Nature (IUCN) Red List of Threatened Species. Pollution; poisoning of our rivers and ponds by chemicals, sewage effluent and agricultural run-

* The word is Romany. I first heard in when we came to the Fens applied to those travellers who are not true Roma.

off; glass eels scooped up before they have any chance to grow to adults in push nets in France, or sold for £750 a kilo in England by people who fish them illegally; eels taken at sea, where it is easy to ignore laws. Human greed will always find a way.

Time was, not long ago, when there would have been many men following Peter's trade. I could have made a friend of him, but our paths only crossed that once in the dark of the moon. (He kept several traditional crafts alive – willow merchant, mole catcher, hedge laying, wildfowling, and net making. I admire that.) The Fens were a major source of supply of eels – fish of all types, in fact – for the towns; and the discomfort of getting your eels in the dark – eels don't like light – and in all weathers, would pay well. They can live a long time out of water if kept moist, and boxes of them live would be sent off to the big towns by rail. Or they might be smoked... delicious. You can do worse than eels.

Peregrinations

To name is to know. I love place names. One of the most thumbed books on my shelves is Ekwall's *Oxford Dictionary of Place Names.* I can be happy for hours with an OS map, reading it almost like a book, working out why this village or that is placed here, deducing something of the land's history from the name. Why is this farm or hamlet called Gibraltar, or Botany Bay, or Little London? Or this drove Knave's Acre? This farm Jerusalem, or New Gant? Why is this parish shaped like this? Why are all these fields in this part so long and thin? (Actually, in some cases I have found out, but I'll spare you (some) or this book will never be finished.)

There was a lady, not without education, who once solemnly warned me that Ely was a funny place, full of witches. I assumed she was referring to the old practices of taper burns on window lintel and fireplace bressumers, or the burying of witchbottles or the inscribing of daisy wheels – the sort of thing that is well documented in books like Enid Porter's *Cambridgeshire Customs & Folklore* (London: Routledge & Kegan Paul, 1969.) 'No', she said, shaking her head earnestly. 'I mean real witches.' Seeing me incredulous or puzzled, she continued, 'It's all there in the place names. Just look! Witchford, Witcham, Coveney.' I changed the subject, tactfully.

But what do those placenames mean? All have stories: 'Witch-' tells us that once upon a time wych elms were a feature at the ford where the little stream from Grunty Fen trickled into the Cove, and of the -ham –'home', or 'village', a few miles away. Coveney is the 'island in the cove or bay' that is now drained as West Fen. Little Thetford is 'people's ford', and indeed there was a Bronze Age track and ford over the river we call the Ouse here. The -port element in Littleport suggests an ancient market; Chettisham is probably the 'ham' of a man called Cetta. Downham is the -ham that sits on the little hill; Wentworth is possibly a 'home inhabited in the winter'. Grunty Fen? Well, complicated – 'obscure', as the books say: Teutonic stem *grunþo* has given rise to Old Norse *grunnr* , *gruðr*, 'shallow, bottom', Swedish *grund*, and the stem *grundu-s* has given Old English *grund*, 'ground,' : *grunting* is perhaps allied to these and may denote a shallow place. It has been suggested that *grunþ* goes back to *grump* and is related to Norwegian *grumen*, 'muddy,' hence 'muddy shallow'…

As you see, one could go on…

But these are all old places, dwelt in by folk long before the strange tongues came from over the sea. What were they called in that distant time? We have only the name of the Ouse to remind us of the speech of those forgotten people.

Street names can delight too. Egremont Street is Agremans Street on the 1610 map by John Speed: is that a personal name like Akerman, or does it suggest sickness, or something to do with an area of land? Why was the present Chapel Street then called Cat Lane? Or a little lane – now called just that – be Causey (causeway? To where? Or Corpse-way) Lane? The name Silver Street might come from the Old English *Selvernestrate* meaning 'of silver' and, indeed, John Stow in his *Survey of London* (1598) remarks that Silver Street in London is 'because of siluer smithes dwelling there' (Ekwall 76; Stow 1:299). Fair enough; but he does say 'I think'. Surely the roads down to the river in Cambridge, or Burwell, or Ely could never have been populated by a luxury trade? A search on the Web turns up a paper published in the *Proceedings* of an Antiquarian Society that tells me, inexplicably, that the origin of the name 'Silver Street' in some towns 'has been ascribed to its association with prostitutes'. Then again, some suggest it is a corruption of *silva*, meaning wood or thicket. Another suggestion is that it refers to the road itself rather than its inhabitants, a folk-image for bad drainage. Just as a Honey Lane is sticky with mud, so a Silver Street has a shining surface because it's perpetually wet and reflects the light. (I am not quite convinced, though it may be significant that Ely's Silver Street was once Fountain Lane.)

Cow Lane is old, older far perhaps than we imagine, for once a lane or road is made, it tends to stay: it is more fuss to move than use. Footsteps pass the door on a hard pavement now, but many more silent ones have passed that way with their joys and sorrows and worries. Down it, as you go down towards the Fen, people perhaps as far back as the Neolithic drove their cattle to summer pasture. It's the nearest convenient walk with the dog, whose frequent pauses to sniff or widdle give plenty of chance to ruminate (not literally...) on where we are, this place all these neighbours, still strangers, accept as just there, while to us it is new in every way. Why is this bend in the road here? Did a neolithic cow wander off the drove and all the others followed?

Halfway down the slope to the Fen, nicely placed where there is water but not too much, excavations in the late 1990s by the Cambridge Archaeological Unit discovered abundant evidence for Middle and Late Saxon and medieval settlement.* For almost 800 years, people lived there, often in the same tofts enclosed by ditches. The site was only finally abandoned, and we do not know why, in the 15th century. The people were not wealthy: no hint of anything like a high-status or even comfortable lifestyle shows. There is no imported pottery, no high-value metalwork, almost no coins. Yet for 24 generations and more it was a stable, gradually evolving settlement, probably supplying food, originally to the monastic settlement Etheldreda founded, then to the abbey, and later to the bishops. All those lives, of people who lived and loved like us, who were passive to the whims and quarrels of the great, of whom we can

---

* Richard Mortimer, Roderick Regan , Sam Lucy, 2005. 'The Saxon and Medieval Settlement at West Fen Road, Ely: the Ashwell Site', *East Anglian Archaeology*, 110 (2005)

know nothing: like T. S. Eliot's women of Canterbury, standing patiently by the Cathedral, in *Murder in the Cathedral.*

Sometimes you get those glimpses across the centuries of the reality of loss and sorrow. I have mourned my unforgotten dogs, and was grateful for their friendship when they were alive. So to hear that among the traces of the settlement were the remains of about 20 dogs, buried carefully in individual graves, while cats and cattle, on the other hand, appear simply to have been dumped in ditches, suddenly makes life in that little village, perhaps 100 people, feel real. The dogs may well have been working dogs, worth their weight in the gold these people did not have, but no matter: they loved them, and grieved when they died.

Up and down Cow Lane for centuries the wagons trundled… hard ground for the wheels at harvest time, a slough in February. These are the people who get no mention save as a class in the writings of the past; these are the people, living the hard, unremitting life of the poor, who made our world possible just as much as the princes and prelates and scholars and sages. Honour them, though they have no memorial.

And the place that knows them no more is now built over, with newish houses that, in general, deferentially tip their hat to the graciousness of the Georgian. But someone in the Council decided that some streets should be given names that recalled (for those who have ears to hear) the history and people of Ely. It was a good decision, and delights me, for it asserts our continuity with those who made the world we take as normal but which they could never have glimpsed. Benedict Street:

101

for the mediaeval Ely monastery was a Benedictine house, and Benedict, Abbott of Monte Cassino, was a great and wise man, whose humane *Rule* is not a bad blueprint for any community, monastic or not; Abbott's way – well, yes, take your pick; Dunstan Street – the reforming Archbishop and friend of the great Athelstan, the first king who could claim to rule all England, and also of Aethelwold, the Bishop of Winchester who refounded the Abbey at Ely; Etheldreda Street – obvious; Christopher Tye Close – not so obvious, but welcome, for he was a good man in terrible times, whose music still is heard in the setting for which he wrote it, the acoustic of which he heard in his head as he wrote; Rifleman's Close, yes, but that needs homework – this is a nice quiet little game you can play as you wait for Milo to finish reading his newspaper of smells. St Ovin's Green – a decent, open, green space with teenage trees that one day may be mighty – oh, how people need those things! – and one of Ely's two PoW camps was near there during WWII, holding Italian prisoners.

But was Ovin a saint? What does that word mean? Who was Ovin? His world, like that of the princess he served, was physically and mentally unimaginably different from ours. Yet he lived and breathed and saw the new greens of an unfolding spring thicken and darken into summer, and saw the first frost of autumn stiffen the grass, and had colds and enjoyed his wine like us. He has a story, but we can only glimpse bits of it, like fragments of the cross that bears his name in the Cathedral he never saw.

The planners wisely – isn't it nice to be nice about them for a change? – have left several open spaces, even some old grown-out hedges. Over one such open space runs an old ditch, delved deep to dry out this tricky soil, and overgrown, where Milo loves to snuffle and sniff. It has been there for much longer than the houses. The new bypass obliterates it just there, but it continues on the other side. For just as the shadows of people long ago press upon the sharp bright present, so too the fields lie sleeping underneath. 'Do not forget us: we are here. One day we shall wake again.'

In an old town like this the pattern of streets often recalls the ancient ways that were there before there were houses: and anyone with any insight knows that, in the scale of things, towns are nearly as temporary as a clearing in a forest.* If you turn away from the river just where ancient Willow Walk meets it, and go past the sewage works, you will cross the little park and children's playground where once was the municipal tip. (Before that, it was a range of mediaeval watercress beds, and watercress still can be found in the ditches of the nearby washes.) Keep going, cross a little bridge over a (usually) dry ditch and you will suddenly find yourself in what could be another time.

Springhead Lane (some call it, perhaps optimistically, Lovers' Lane) is palpably old. It is especially beloved of dogwalkers, and Milo has often in his youthful enthusiasm (that has not always been welcomed) started conversations. You can feel the age before you start to do

---

* Indeed, in grid-planned New York or Atlanta there are gently sinuous streets, Broadway and Peach Tree, which were Native American trails long before the settlers came.

the usual rule of thumb things like estimating the age of the grown-out hedges that flank it, and spread over its ditches, by counting the species of woody plants in them. It goes, now, from nowhere in particular to nowhere in particular – though its name crosses the road and climbs up the bluff of the isle as if making for one of the old mills that were on that ridge. Its course, if continued, would take it into the middle of Sainsbury's, a supermarket built with the intelligent ideas of being on stilts so cars could park in the shade – and save land – and of covering the roof with enough solar panels, they say, to boil every kettle in Ely. In the other direction, well, its line peters out in the water of Roswell Pits. But the few minutes' length has once been metalled – someone thought that worthwhile – and it is wide enough to take a cart, and I am pretty certain it is one of the major old routes into the town. Now it is just the haunt of dogwalkers, joggers, and perhaps the occasional lover. On the one side is an open meadow, on the other a grazed field and the smaller of the Pits. As dusk falls, time pauses as a barn owl ghosts over the meadow silently on its fimbriate wings: this is what the people who made this track would have seen and not heard.

Nature comes back with a vengeance. The little trees on each side of the path have had a good summer, and have reached out to tell each other about it. Over August the trees had made the track palpably narrower, reaching out with feelers that clutched your clothes as you walked two abreast: 'Here we are. Don't ignore us. We were here before you.' A couple more years, and the lane would be a long thicket. It does not take long. Near where my son's family live in Hampshire is a lane to the village that has been there for, I think, millennia. In latter years it was kept open only by the gamekeeper's tractor flail, but has been neglected for only three years. The dogs and I walk in single file. Next year I shall not be able to follow that way, worn deep into the landscape by the countless feet of long-gone men and animals. But the hollow in the hillside will be there.

And even in the heart of the town… Back in the village, taking the current dog out for his last slow widdle and squat before bed, I always expected to notice and hear things in the quieter world, especially on a windless night when the trees were quiet. A muntjac deer barking; an owl; something rustling in the undergrowth. It's easy to assume that the last walk in a town will offer no such hints of other creatures going about their business, caring little for us except to keep out of our bothersome way. But you get surprises: even on pavement and in streetlight expect the unexpected. On Milo's slow, late night walks around Cow Lane – slow because he sniffs everything for news, and there seem to be much more than in the village, and it would be impolite to hurry him just as I hate to be interrupted when I am reading – we hear owls, usually tawny, or very occasionally the harsh bark of a muntjac. Signs – and smells – and occasional sightings remind you that foxes rather enjoy town life. On the eve of Bin Days the occasional enterprising rat is glimpsed. But so do other more unexpected creatures. Near the allotment there is a row of little dwellings for elderly people, with a small patch of grass in front of them. One kindly lady regularly puts out bowls of food and water by the door for the many cats that dispute this territory, sometimes cacophonously. They crouch under parked cars, staring balefully at Milo as he goes past. But sometimes when I turn that corner at night I hear a snuffling, and sure enough, there is the hedgehog coming to tuck in to his free meal, with no fear of marauding badger to disturb his feast. (Badgers are one of the few animals that can open up a spiky curled-up hedgehog for dinner: which is one reason why they are getting so scarce, as the badger population increases.) Is it one hedgehog or several, serially? It would be very interesting to know the density of this secret life we do not really notice. It is, I suspect, much greater than we imagine.

The fields lie sleeping underneath the town. Just waiting for us to finish.

It is sometimes a job keeping Milo away from the proffered cat food. He has no idea of manners.

Getting About

The first house I ever entered in Ely was an imposing Georgian house on St Mary's Street. As the door was opened to me by the maid I saw the stairs up from the hall had the blue plush carpet held neatly by the first polished brass stair rods my youth had seen. I was impressed. I was about 25, Arts Editor for a publishing house, and I was calling on one of our authors, the Classicist Dr Bertha Tilley, who happened to be a very distinguished Head of Ely High School for Girls, once just a few yards further down the street. (During her 30 years as Head it had moved to larger premises on the outskirts of the city.) I was there to see her about an edition of Virgil she was preparing – schoolteachers had time to do serious scholarship then – and I was a bit in awe of this woman who had written the standard work on the countryside of the Latium Virgil knew. (She went on, much later, with me as her editor, to do a distinguished edited selection from the 'How To' agricultural manual of the seriously rich Roman scholar Marcus Terentius Varro. He tells you to treat your slaves well, for they are valuable property.) Bertha became a friend, and gradually I came to realise how influential she had been on so many women in the town and its neighbourhood, and how in her school she sought the very highest standards of and for her girls, which was then of course selective. (The 11+ exam was introduced by the Butler Education Act of 1944, and she had been in post when that huge change arrived.) She passionately deplored the forced introduction of comprehensive schools, to which her own beloved school had to conform. I think of her often; and of Sybil Marshall, her neighbour a few doors down, another fine educationalist (in her case, primary) whose books and work profoundly influenced my own thinking about what education was for.

When our children were old enough and Jenny was able to go back part-time to work, Bertha gave her a job at the High School. It was a happy partnership, despite the grind of having to get there and back by bus from Reach every day – you could do that then – however grim the morning or dark the evening winter lanes. She enjoyed the work, and teaching the girls, and one story she told emphasised the cultural and social mix the 11+ generated. A girl in her class, very bright, had won a school prize. Jenny asked her to choose a book she would like to have presented to her in Assembly. The girl, from a farm way down the Fen, replied, 'No, Miss, I don't want one of them, thank you. You see, we've already got one of them at home.'

Never think people are simple. Outwardly, Bertha was the very type of everyone's idea of a Headmistress. But underneath… well, she never married, and when she was editing Virgil's great tragic fourth book of the *Aeneid*, which tells the story of the doomed affair of Aeneas and Dido, she wrote movingly, with real passion and feeling, about the predicament of a woman who had given everything, and had been abandoned. I never asked, of course.

If you walk along St Mary's Street, you pass Bedford House, which had housed Bertha's Ely High School for Girls from 1905 to 1957. The elegant triple-pile Georgian house had been built for the Bedford Level Corporation, which was responsible for the fen drainage which changed everything. You will be tracing the route by which many mediaeval travellers would have arrived, following the boundary wall of the monastery precincts.[10] Roughly at the Lamb Hotel, you turn into what was Stepil Lane: the High Street, with a sixteenth century gatehouse to remind you of the monastic enclosure. The first Lamb Inn was there in the fifteenth century: then it would have been the 'Lamb and Flag'. Its sign would have shown a lamb, carrying a white flag with a red cross on it: the symbol of Christ as the sacrificial Lamb of God and of His resurrection. In some parts where Reform was strong this was felt to tend too much to Rome, and some inn names were shortened to just 'The Lamb'.[11] Much later, the old inn began to do rather well in the eighteenth century with the building of toll roads – turnpikes like the one William Gilpin used – leading from Cambridge to the port of Lynn and the increasingly prosperous drained Fenland. Ely became a regular stopping place for changing post horses, and later for the newfangled stagecoaches. It did, in fact, very well indeed, and the owner became very rich and could do all sorts of elegant remodelling things to the building.

As you will have guessed by now, when I walk through an old town, I am often in my mind walking through what is not there any more. This habit, I admit, can be an inconvenience to fellow pedestrians and the occasional motorist. Archways, sometimes filled in with brick, remind that once they led back to stabling for horses, and how noisy horse-drawn traffic was, with the iron of hoof and wheelrim on the cobbles. (And the amount of dung to be cleared up.) My mother, born in 1901, remembered straw being put down outside a house to deaden the noise where someone was ill. I often lift my eyes to first floor level and glimpse another era. For example: the Ovaltine girl smiling wholesomely from an end wall in the Mile End Road in London; or, in Cambridge as you come down Castle Hill, just where you will see it as you trundle down on your bicycle to the Great Bridge over the Cam, faded paint high on a wall tells you that the owner of that establishment is 'Licensed to Let a Horse and Gig'. And you start to ruminate: licensed by whom? At that date (to judge by the lettering) it must have been the University Proctors, for a horse and gig was the sort of thing a flashy nineteenth century undergraduate might hire to cut a dash. Or on Hills Road, built up after Cambridge's new railway station drew development towards it, a side wall has a bull's head painted on it to remind you that this

was the home of 'BULL'S DAIRIES': long, long gone
now, and only the joke remains. In Ely's wide Market
Street – wideness that reminds you that here there *was*
a market – on an old shop that is now a Thai restaurant,
is a (re)painted advertisement that brings back memory
of a time, not that long ago, before the railways changed
the world, when the Lamb Inn was on a key transport
network:

LYNN, CAMBRIDGE and LONDON
VANS, FLY and STAGE WAGGON
To the BULL INN, *BISHOPSGATE STREET*
EVERY DAY
ISAAC MARSH and WILLIAM SWAN
PROPRIETORS

Ely is a natural stopping place on the road between
Cambridge and Lynn when people travelled on foot, on
horseback or, later and faster, by the stagecoaches that
made use of the new toll roads. Increasingly there was
demand for accommodation, and for a supply of fresh
horses (which had to be kept at the stages), and the
proprietor of The Lamb was happy to provide.

The trade of coachman was a very skilled one, and
attracted some unusual people; and gentleman amateurs[12]
with time and money on their hands. By chance I came
across a curious book of memoirs, *The Autobiography of
a Stage Coachman*, published in 1845, by Thomas Cross,
one of the drivers of the Lynn stage. He had some
education and some literary ambition. When he lost his
job as a stagecoachman because of the railways, he made
a sort of living by selling his own poetical compositions

of a religious and historical kind. They had some merit, and attracted the attention in Cambridge of dons and undergraduates. In 1853 Joseph Romilly, the Registrary of the University, recorded in his diary,

> *Cross the Coachman called upon me and showed himself a very great fool. He wished me to obtain for him the means of seeing the Prince [Consort, then Chancellor of the University] that he might remind him of the Poems he had sent him (handsomely bound): I told him that it was altogether out of the question ... Might he call on Dr Whewell [Master of Trinity College] about the business? I most strongly dissuaded so rash a piece of impertinence: I afterward learned from Lucy that this cidevant coachman bears a very bad character and has been 4 times in prison! He is a candidate for a place in the Fitzwilliam Museum...*

His book is worth reading, and he was actually no fool: In 1855, four years after this bitchy note of Romilly's – par for his course – he was runner up to the man who was appointed to the new post of Town Librarian of Cambridge. Some, indeed, thought well of him. But to return: three times a week 'The Union' stagecoach ran from King's Lynn to Ely to Cambridge. Cross usually stopped in Cambridge, but one snowy night he was forced to stop at The Lamb. He had mixed feelings about The Lamb: he says that in all the time he used to stop at the Lamb the only meal ever offered to him was spatchcocked eels and mutton chops. He disliked the small bar, where a bag of lemons (for making punch) hung from the ceiling. They were mouldy. He thought the sherry fiery, but the port was decent.

That snowy night, his passengers were cosy sitting around the fire, when a servant came in and asked them to come upstairs to see one of their fellow travellers. Cross says:

> '*On ascending the stars and entering the room we beheld a fine matronly lady habited as a Quakeress seated at the table with the book before her. She stated that as chance had thrown us together, she thought a few words from the Book of Life would not be unacceptable and accordingly read us some passages. She dismissed us with an extempore prayer, wishing the blessing and mercy of the Almighty*'.

That lady was Elizabeth Fry, one of the first and one of the greatest proponents of reform of the prison system, especially for women. She was born in 1780, so she might have been about 60 at the date of this encounter. She came of a prominent Norfolk banking family, the Gurneys, who became such a byword for wealth and honesty that W. S. Gilbert can refer to being 'as rich as the Gurneys' in the Judge's Song in *Trial by Jury* (1875). They were also very influential in the anti-slavery movement. Elizabeth married, when she was 20, Joseph Fry, another Quaker from another banking family, based in Bristol: a family whose chief memorial now is chocolate. They had 11 children. Poor things, they came too early for the Chocolate Creams that gladdened my youthful heart.

Of course, three or four generations ago, when people travelled more slowly and more laboriously, often on foot, there were pubs and inns spaced pretty regularly along the roads. They were needed, giving shelter on a foul day or night, and refreshment on a hot summer one. Some on the trunk roads made themselves into the roadhouses so fashionable in the 1920s and 30s among the Bright Young Things with money and cars. Most, especially off the major routes, did not. Again, the once ubiquitous Railway Inn or Hotel, with the destruction of the branch line network by Dr Beeching, with its *raison d'être* removed, now scratches a living if it survives at all, or is converted into a house 'with an interesting history'.

Railways: here was the paradigm shift that changed so much. They were not always welcomed, by any means, and for all sorts of reasons. The University in Cambridge, extremely powerful in the town and dominating the Town Council, had quite a number of senior members who were determined to stop it as it would offer so many opportunities for the young gentlemen to corrupt their morals by easy access to London's fleshpots. Indeed, the fleshpots might come to Cambridge: they did not quite envisage the Friday Popsy Express (17.36 from Liverpool Street) as it was called, of my youth, which disgorged lots of fiancées, and others, come to Cambridge for the weekend. But if they had seen it, they might have said 'We told you so!' In 1843 *The Railway Times* (Vol. 6, p. 507ff.) reported a heated debate about the advisability and profitability of bringing the line from London, already as far as Bishop's Stortford, to Cambridge. In 1844 the then Vice Chancellor, Robert Phelps, wrote to the Directors of the Eastern Counties Railway about their proposal to run excursion trains to Cambridge on Sundays

'with the object of attracting foreigners and undesirable characters to the University of Cambridge on that sacred day. The Vice Chancellor of the University of Cambridge wishes to point out to the directors of the Eastern Counties Railway that such a proceeding would be as displeasing to Almighty God as it is to the Vice Chancellor of the University of Cambridge.'

The University successfully blocked attempts by the different railway companies to have their own stations, forcing them to use just one, and equally successfully blocked the plan for a central railway station on the Backs. The motive was less aesthetic than making access more difficult for the young men to get to the London trains. Eventually, a site for the station a good mile from Great St Mary's was chosen, out in the fields. The beautiful and imposing station, a tasteful echo of the Ospitale degli Innocenti in Florence, however, drew Cambridge to itself, as new streets of houses were laid out towards it and the New Town was developed: with skill and some taste. The station still has something of style amid the turgid mediocrity that now surrounds it. I wish I had seen it when the *porte cochère* was still open and cabs drew up on the cobbles under its shelter.

No, not always welcome. It brought one sort of employment, it killed another, long familiar, sort of employment, and most people do not like change. Reach, for example, as a village had done very well out of the water trade. But when Squire Charles Peter Allix, a major shareholder in the company that built the Cambridge to Mildenhall line, insisted that the station be built at the bottom of his park at Swaffham Prior and not at the commercially important centre, Reach, the water trade collapsed, and Reach began its long decline: no new houses between the 1870s and the council houses of the 1950s, and a population that in 1900 had been over 500 down to about 200 in the 1950s. And the six or seven pubs and alehouses of the glory days reduced to one, where Wilfrid the owner stood mournfully at the bar in his flat cap with his cup of tea, gloomily telling thirsty hopefuls that Steward and Patterson of Ely had not sent any bitter this month, but he still had the remains of a barrel of mild.

But deep in the Fens, on the soft and unstable soils, building railways was not easy, and the need for water transport, especially in sugar beet season, remained. Accidents happened on the new lines, and people were not slow to draw moral lessons. In the cloister of the Cathedral a sandstone slab remembers Willam Pickering and Richard Edger, who were killed in a railway accident on the Ely to Norwich line on Christmas Eve 1845, with the inscription of what was later printed as a broadside ballad, 'The Spiritual Railway':

The line to Heaven by Christ was made,
With heavenly truth the Rails are laid,
From Earth to Heaven the Line extends,
To Life Eternal where it ends.
Repentance is the Station then,

Where Passengers are taken in ;
No Fee for them is there to pay,
For Jesus is himself the way.
God's Word is the first Engineer,
It points the way to Heaven so clear,
Through tunnels dark and dreary here.
It does the way to Glory steer.
God's Love the fire, his Truth the Steam,
Which drives the Engine and the Train;
All you who would to Glory ride,
Must come to Christ, in him abide.
In First, and Second, and Third Class,
Repentance, Faith, and Holiness,
You must the way to Glory gain,
Or you with Christ will not remain.
Come then poor Sinners, now's the time,
At any Station on the Line,
If you'll repent, and turn from sin,
The Train will stop and take you in.

Nicholas Pevsner (*The Buildings of England: Cambridgeshire*, 365), commented that it is 'eminently characteristic of the earnestness with which this new triumph of human ingenuity was still regarded'.

Oak, Willow, Stone

E ly, July, 2022. We have been partly living in Rosanna's
Ely house for some six months now, and we wake
early, for it is hard to sleep in the hottest, driest summer
here anyone under 50 can remember. Not a breath of air
is stirring as I leave the house. (The last time it was this
hot here I was 19 degrees of latitude away from droughty
England, hauling a sledge across the Spitsbergen icecap...
Could do with a bit of that now.) The grass on Palace
Green, usually so coolly green against the mellow brick of
the palace Bishop Alcock built at the end of the 1400s, is
baked to the colour of a savannah. It is still early. But there
was no dew on the grass even at dawn – there has not been
for weeks, for this summer has been so unrelentingly dry.
Near the rubbish bin, just by where the winos sit under the
trees, there is a carrion crow, its wings half spread, open

beaked, its pink tongue arched, panting. Black feathers take up the heat of the early morning sun. Not a bird I like especially, but I am sorry for it. It hardly moves as I walk past, close. Poor thing.

The grey cliff of the West Front of the Cathedral soars up, rebuffing the waves of heat. You look up at layer on layer of subtly changing ways of doing the Romanesque – for there were several lodges of masons, each knowing their own right way to do it, who in successive campaigns built it all those years ago. (Yet that's a mere blink in time's eye...) Its morning shade is a blessing. I catch the shrill call of the peregrines who are nesting high up on the south transept, but don't see them. They are most welcome new residents, for when I first came to these parts from the green north of Lancashire you never saw raptors: the pesticides of industrial farming had almost wiped them out. Now the webcam trained on their nest high up on the Cathedral allows so many of us delightedly to watch a sort of soap opera, an avian Archers, an Everyday Story of Predatory Folk.

Oak

The (almost) coolth of the Galilee porch is welcome, and the harsh brightness of the light is softened. Out of nowhere the thought suddenly comes that here, once, pilgrims to Etheldreda's shrine sat on the stone benches at the sides and took off their filthy shoes and washed their feet: the floor slopes very gently to the west to let the water run out. I push hard to open the little wicket in the great oak West doors and the expected rush of air into the nave through the gap does not disappoint. Once, to step into this nave – 'the coldest place in England', my mother used to say – in high summer demanded an extra sweater, and in winter, even with the magnificent old cast iron Gurney stoves going full belt, gloves and thick socks were advisable. Nowadays, it's heated much more comfortably for a much more pampered generation. Today I would have been glad of a bit of the old chill.

I always pause here, if I am alone, to take in the majesty of the nave reaching far down to the screen, and then beyond, to the eastern windows. And if nobody is looking, I tread the labyrinth. Most churches of note in the Middle Ages had one by the west door, symbol of the complexity of our life journey, for which our progress down the nave from baptistery to – well, what? – becomes metaphor. If you look up, you see the fine ceiling designed by Henry Le Strange, which is designed to lead your mind – if you can ignore the crick in your neck – from Creation to Last Judgement. But early though it is, I do have company, and that is not why I have come anyway.

I forget myself. I have not told you why I am here, in this much loved building. Not this time is it for one of my rare attendances at the early Eucharist – I still call that, in the old phrase, the Morrow Mass. I am here to visit a corpse – or, rather, part of one. It lies for the time being in the North Aisle, through the massive Romanesque arcade.

It is far, far bigger than I expected. Many long yards of polished wood have been shaped and planed into a table, and it has just arrived here. The body of the tree fell perhaps five thousand years ago – it was probably already dead, smothered, its roots unable to breathe for the gradual rising of the sea and the consequent waterlogging of the sustaining soil by the ponding back of the slow rivers.

Quite quickly (in vegetable time) the blanket of peat grew round the supine corpse, sealing its heartwood from air and rot. Thousands of its fellows, standing shoulder to shoulder, met the same fate. People think a great wind from the North West felled those who outfaced it on the faraway edge of the forest, and they in turn with the gale's aid pushed over those behind them, all to lie the same way. We saw this again in 1987, where a whole living wood could be uprooted in a few short hours. I think of the lost, graceful beeches of Wandlebury Ring, catching the sunlight on the shine of their leaves, or the parade of 50 year old oaklings along the drive at beloved Felbrigg which that wind blew down. But there was one big difference between those trees and the community of noble oaks and beeches to which this tree belonged.

For this fragment, dug up in a bog in Norfolk, is from a tree far, far taller than any oak, however old, in England now. Its straight grain, knotless from so few side branches, shows it grew close in community with its fellows, siblings perhaps, in what a poet friend of mine calls the dark fierce freedom of trees. Trees make the air we breathe, they exhale so we can inhale. The Tree stretched itself up to the sun, as tall as some of the younger redwoods on the other side of the world, grasping the power of sunlight with its leaves to fuel its alchemy of chlorophyll. (It was a minor delight to learn that the chlorophyll molecule, based on magnesium, has an identical pattern to our own haemoglobin, based on iron.) And on the unbroken canopy of the forest the sun played, and rain fell, and the wood grew and made a home and habitation for many creatures for whom its massiveness was a whole world. When this tree was a stripling, as once it unimaginably was, there were few men in this land, and few cattle to graze away the seedlings, and the wildwood reached beyond imagining, away across where the grey waves of the North Sea now cover the way over Doggerland to Germany and beyond.

This bit of the once living body is now a table, a table longer than any frightened Russian tyrant could desire, a table ideal for community, and feasting, and singing after supper, and gladsomeness. Look at the sheen the craft of man has polished on it, and you see reflected ages of memory, and long, slow steady thinking. It lies as if sleekly asleep, waiting to wake up to the talk of men and women who would sit around it to feast, creatures of the moment, only slightly longer living by this tree's reckoning than the insects and birds that made its canopy of leaves alive with the noises of summer, the song-challenges of birds marking territory, the plash of water shaking the outstretched leaves in a grateful shower, the buzz of insects in the tree's graciousness.

Where would we be without trees? Even dead they are all around, as books, furniture, houses… what could we do without them? Once this grain ran between root tip – who knows what messages they carry? – and leaf tip, and sap coursed between the vibrant community of the soil and the energy of sky. The tree had time to grow, lots and lots of it, and we can read in it the varying of the seasons of the past and the times Gaia burped and let off a little volcano. But – unimaginable thought – once it was an acorn. It had a parent reaching back almost to when no man was in this land and the land rawly remembered the ice that had covered it. It has seen stone turned into tool, and brown bronze come, and the grey sheen of iron

– all fell indeed to trees, as man grasps the wildwood for his own and the community of trees falls one by one, and pasture and field reach to the once unseen horizon. But this tree escaped that fate. It was already mummy in the marsh, and felt no blow of axe and wedge and beetle, bore no burning of brashings.

The polished table is a lovely thing. Not alive – or not in our usual sense – any more: a relic to which people make pilgrimage. The cells of its wood formed when we were few, and so many of the choices that have made our world since, one leading ineluctably to another, precluding some, forcing others, were yet to be made. On this table is our history, our family tree, if we can learn how to read it. For about one thing a long life has given me certainty: the ever-presentness of the past.

You will gather I love trees, and reverence the work they do for us. I love wood too, the smells and texture and sounds of different woods, their different uses – in the old economy, to make a wheel, say, you needed three woods: unsplittable elm for the nave, the straight strength of ash for the spokes, and the toughness of beech for the fellies. To build one of the lighters and barges that worked these Fen waterways, you needed grown oak knees for strength, and elm planking because elm in water does not rot – which is why the Romans used hollowed out elm trunks, laid thick end to thin end, for buried water pipes. (That is why we talk about 'trunking' in all sorts of contexts, even roads.)

Of course, trees *don't* do things for us, mere creatures of the moment, but simply for themselves. Even so, they are part of the same web of life as us, and everything affects everything else, both horizontally, so to speak, and vertically in time. So some gratitude does no harm. This will not be the last time in this book, if I ever can bring myself to finish it, when trees and woodland will appear, from the ancient oaks of Keskadale or the Martindale Yew to the spreading, lazy grey willow in Coley's Meadow by the slow river near the house at Reach – and the mighty oaks that made the Octagon of the Cathedral. But there are other things to talk about in this ramble of a book: for one, that seismic but not unwelcome slow uprooting of this old stick in the mud from the old house by the Fen he had inhabited for sixty years and his putting down roots in that even older house in the city that stands on the island. The journey, real and metaphorical, between those two places, carries so much baggage with it, memories of people, places, ideas, passions, griefs. There is the delight in getting to see a new place in, shall we say, stereo: not just a handsome, even beautiful, town *now*, which you visit, but a place ghosted with the dark and light things that happened there, where the echoes have not died away, if you have ears to hear. But enough: the Table was not the first ancient oak whose cadaver I have met, though it would have been by far the noblest if I had seen even its bones in their outlining of its glory.

That first bog oak I dismembered... With a borrowed McCormick tractor I dragged its 30 foot trunk – a pigmy, really! – up from the field in the Fen where it had slept for centuries until a ploughshare hit it. I got it to the river bank behind the garden, and now had to get it to bits. The first job was to split the tree lengthwise, and for reeving, said old Seth, our neighbour who scorned my greenness but was ever ready with help and advice, I needed wedges and a sledge. I had neither...

Seth pottered about in his sheds, built of planks of bog oak roughly split, and found me the head of a sledgehammer that only needed the fitting of a new hickory shaft, some bits of a cart axle, and part of the chassis of an old Riley, and off he had us go in our dilapidated Morris Traveller (some of the woodwork, ash, was rotting quite noticeably) early one morning to his friend in Lode who still kept his smithy going, just. His work now was mostly shoeing ponies for the increasing numbers of young girls whose parents, often incomers, could afford animals that the old folk looked at contemptuously as 'bloody useless on the land.' Bill lit a bit of newspaper and thrust it into the cold bed of smithy nuts – anthracite – and started pumping the bellows. Within minutes a good, smokeless fire was going and taking the morning chill off the shed. Soon the heart of it was white, and Bill methodically took the bits of old iron in his pincers, heated them till they were white hot, and beat them on the anvil standing on its round of oak trunk, the sparks flying, and heated them again and beat them again, and soon we had four good wedges. I have them still, their tops curly-edged where my sledge hammer has punished them over the years. I must have been one of the last people to see a village smith working at his forge, the walls hung around with the bits of his trade – iron tyres for cart wheels, blanks hung on the beams for shoes for the heavy horses the land would never see again, and in the yard the tank in which the hot metal from the forge used to be tempered.

125

Obviously, when splitting a trunk you start at the end away from the involved grain of the roots – as the gap widens, it exerts more force on the part where you will not easily split it – or saw it, for that matter. The outer wood was soft enough: still wet, it broke off in lumps and the wedges had nothing on which to bite. Seth stood, saying nothing, rolling a cigarette in his hands: Rizla paper taken from the green packet, tobacco from his pouch, rolled between the fingers of his right hand, slowly lick the gummed edge of the paper… watching me get crosser and crosser. He enjoyed that. The cigarette went out. He lit it again.

In the end he stepped in. He walked back up the lane without saying anything, and came back with an adze. And two strokes along the grain cleared the soft wood and cut down to the hard stuff. He stood back. He was determined I was going to learn how to do it. 'There'. Nothing more. I hold the wedge with one hand and tap it gently with the sledge in the other. It stays there, its sharp new edge just buried in the wood. Good. I lift the sledge high and bring it crashing down as hard as I can. It misses the wedge and bounces on the wood. The wedge jumps out onto the grass. Seth lights his fag with a flare from the huge old petrol lighter he has had since the First War. Repeat. This time I hit the wedge. It bounces out. Then he speaks. 'Too much of an 'urry, mate. Little taps do the job.' Good advice… little taps… the wedge goes in, millimeter by millimeter, and a tiny crack appears, bleeding water that has been hidden in that wood for thousands of years. Hit it a bit more, still quite gently, and the crack runs a bit. The wedge is now well embedded, and you could not pull it out. Seth:

'Now do yew give un a good welt'. Yes: hard, sledge hammer way above my head. The crack widens. Seth: 'Do yew wait till yew hears that wood talking.' And sure enough, there is a creaking, a groan, as if something (Ariel?) is trying to get out. In with another wedge, where the crack is narrower, and the wood talks, and the first wedge lifts out easily from the split, and another wedge goes in further down, and soon the trunk has been broken out of the round: always the hardest one to do. I am tired, know I shall be stiff on the morrow, but to old Seth this is work he would not leave unfinished, and he keeps me at it until the trunk is split – riven – into six long lengths. It is his teatime, and off he goes, leaving me with hands sore and jarred from the shock of the sledge on the wedges, and aching arms.

Ernie goes past on the McCormick: 'Getting it to bits then? Yew gets hot three times with that old wood: yew gets hot splitting, then sawing, then burning it. Good value that is.' It will still have to be sawn into logs that will fit the fire … I had not thought of that.

We began with an old two handed saw Seth had given me and recently taught me how to sharpen and set: his saw set still sits on a shelf in the stable. In the end, Don – slow, ruminative Don, who would always be complaining that either the land 'wor too wet to goo on' or 'her's too dry' – went past and took pity on us. He brought his blue Fordson tractor to where the tree lay and rigged up a long drive belt from the power takeoff to run his bench saw – a fearsome thing, with no guards, of course. We had the lengths cut into logs in a day. (Then of course we had to carry it and stack it in the garden – we earned our winter heat.)

The wood, black as dull coal, seemed almost too beautiful to burn as its grain saw the light it had never seen. Nowadays it would have been shaped and polished into beautiful things. But we burned its millennia of memory of sun and water and soil, and added to the winter smell of the village, and it kept us warm – at least our fronts – with a slow red glow, an occasional little clear blue flame, and left a soft ochre ash which went on the vegetable patch. That tree lasted us a winter, until the west wind came with the promise of spring.

It's when you look at a mature tree and realise that, without your noticing, *that* is the sapling or cutting or acorn or nut you stuck in the ground, that you realise how long you have been in a place – rather like the point in life when, as we used to say, the policemen look young and autumn will come soon. Now, perhaps, it is the politicians who look (and behave) like some of the more wet behind the ears youths I have spent my life teaching. (Except I get fond of the latter.) I have planted a lot of trees in and around the village which have survived all that agrochemicals and machinery and drought have thrown at them and are mature, fruitful – and beautiful. I am as proud of that as of anything in my life. One of them, now decades old, in the garden, grew from an acorn I gathered in the Lyth Valley in what was then Lancashire Over The Sands, where the damson orchards, foaming in blossom in spring, flow down to the flats by the beloved estuary of the Kent I know so well. And there is one oak by the river, pedunculate, who is a special friend. I knew him as a mere sapling, but his generous boughs are now low and spreading, for he has grown these forty years with no competition. Our dogs have always loved his discreet shade for their own doggy reasons.

It is hard to leave my trees. Better plant some more.

In 1322 the Norman tower at the central crossing of the Cathedral collapsed.[13] Too much weight had been placed on the four piers on which it stood. Such things, and worse, happened, and would continue to happen as ambitions of the newer Gothic style pushed the limits of the possible in height further and further: the entire nave of Beauvais Cathedral, only completed twelve years before, collapsed in 1284. There was never money to replace it.

What to do? Prior Crauden seems to have been adept at persuading the Crown to cough up money, Bishop Hotham was of noted generosity, and the Sacrist, Alan of Walsingham, who was overseeing John of Wisbech's building of the spectacular Lady Chapel, was something of an administrative genius.[14] He realised that a mere rebuilding might well end with the same result. So he made the crucial decision to abandon a square crossing, and go for an octagon in wood, carried on eight great piers. This meant cutting back into the Norman stonework of the nave, transepts and choir, which very noticeably (if you are not looking up at the wonder of the Octagon) disrupts the stately rhythm of the nave arcade. (You might notice on the new column on the north a ghost of the mediaeval paint that once was background to a statue of a saint.)

William Hurley, who became Edward III's King's Carpenter, who did work at the Tower, Windsor and the old palace of Westminster, was the man who solved the problem of the 70 foot span being way beyond what any available timber could span. (The Methusaleh oaks of the Table were no more.)* His solution was an outer wooden octagon, painted to resemble the eight new stone piers, completed about 1328, which supported it. From this a timber vault carried a higher, smaller octagon, on which the lantern was constructed of eight massive vertical timber piers. He had a height of some 60 feet[15] to deal with, and oaks that big – mere pigmies compared to The Oak of The Table – were rare even in 1328 and are unknown now. They needed to trim to a sapless scantling of 3ft 4ins × 2ft 8ins. The oaks had to be bought, and then brought, from Chicksands Priory in Bedfordshire: Alan went down there with Hurley to inspect them. Once the oxen had lugged them down to the little river Ivel, which runs into the Ouse at Tempsford, they could be brought to the foot of Ely's hill by water, dragged up the hill and resurrected into mathematical and architectural glory. And at the centre of the timber vault which these giants support – mere youths as trees go – John of Burwell carved for the boss a magnificent Christ in Majesty, looking down on all that he had made and blessing it, for He saw that it was good.

Half an hour, they say... well, the last time we went up to the Octagon there was only the very learned guide with us, and we were the last tour of the day. It was deep calling to deep: there was just so much to talk

---

* I am told the design owes something to Islamic precedent. There was a good deal of cross cultural borrowing of good ideas.

about and discuss, that we spent a good hour and more together, and I would have wished it longer. I shall ever be grateful. You walk across the lead of the presbytery roof to a little door that leads to the unseen innards of the great structure. Prosaically, a dustpan and brush was on the floor just inside, for people do come up here frequently. Black with age, the great timber supporters of the massive trunks were all around, and the adze marks that someone had made in the 1320s were as fresh and sharp as when the blade smote the wood when it was the golden of new oak. One adze had had a nick in its blade: the mark in the wood is clear. Graffiti of all dates and none... Carpenters' marks. The forebears felt very close. (Did they wear the equivalent of hard hats, now obligatory even for politicians safely visiting factories for photo opportunities, men digging up the road at their feet, or archaeologists crouched over the ground – lest the sky fall on their heads? I doubt it.)

And then the surprise, and the delight: below the uppermost widows, which fracture the white light of Heaven into the stories the stained glass tells, are 32 panels, each painted with an angel playing an instrument in the unceasing consort of Heaven. These swing open, and you look down the dizzying distance to the floor below, where little people move about unaware of your regard. It is a curious and humbling feeling, for you will go down to be one of them again, and not know who regards you. The mediaeval angels have had the paint that gives them 'being' touched up, of course, and, close to, the brushwork and colouring is less subtle than you expect: but then, at the distance from which they are usually seen, that does not matter.

On high days and Holidays – literally, in the old sense!
– the panels are opened and the choristers can sing the
songs the angels sing from on high, joining their voices
to those here below. I have never heard it, but I will one
day. But I have heard the double choir of St Mark's in
Venice singing Gabrieli from the high places of that great
building. *Gloria in excelsis...*

And so down the steep steps, across the roof leads
in the chilly wind, and down into the everyday. Tea and
the prosaic called. But those adze marks... I can hear the
'plunk' of the tool in my head, the good steel honed to a
biting sharpness, and imagine the knotted muscles as the
tool is lifted for the next stroke. Man's sweat made that
miracle happen.

I shall plant my little oakling where the routine
lawnmower or brush cutter will not find it until...

Willow

Things surface like seedlings out of the mould of the
mind, thrusting up out of the litter of many autumns. Just
so the land asserts itself: 'Do not ignore me. I am here.
There are some things you cannot change.' When did I
first notice the differences between osiers and willows and
sallows, plants of this wet country you take for granted?
And get to know what each was good for?

When we first went to the house at Reach, there was
an old Prince Albert apple tree down on the river bank,
by the corrugated iron privy. The privy was redundant,
though in good order (and useful for tools). There was
no other shelter from the searching winter winds that

came off the fen. Something had to be done, for in February the local folk called those north-easterlies lazy winds, because they did not go round but took a short cut through you. Seth, as usual had the answer: 'Yew plant a line of ozhyers; soon have a hedge.' Sure enough: a cutting of Osier (*Salix viminalis* – the Latin *vimen* = pliant twig) stuck in January in moist ground – it loves, indeed demands dampness – will strike root and be a bush in no time. So we did: and soon heard the wind sing in it. As it happens, it's a grand habitat for small creatures, and they say it can even decontaminate the soils on which it is planted, so it can be used with reeds in filter beds for natural sewage systems. Like all its European cousins, it has been here since the ice melted.

Most of the *salix* family strike easily. In January, you can drive stakes of grey willow into the ground to hold three strands of barbed wire to keep the stock in. No matter if the stakes rot, for there's plenty more where that fast-growing wood came from. But most often, if the ground is damp, it strikes, and before you know where you are, you have trees that need pollarding – and stock will eat the smaller brashings. There were three big grey willows along the track behind the house in Reach which Young Albert remembered cutting as fence posts. Each August the sheep in Coley's meadow by the river ruminated in the shade of a willow thicket – all one tree, actually – that had started as a post, grown to be a tree, had split and half fallen in a gale, and taken root, and done it again, and again and again, until it reaches a quarter of the way across the field. Useful wood, and well dried it was much prized in the later Middle Ages for a quick, bright fire ladies might have in their smart chambers with the newfangled chimneys. And out of its wood you can make many useful things.

Oh yes, far more useful than just a windbreak. And ubiquitous wherever there is water. The wet, often flooded fens of eastern England, like the Somerset Levels, were ideal for willows and osiers, which grow magnificently when allowed to, and the osiers were a crop of major importance well into the 1900s. Indeed, it used to be said that so valuable was the yearly crop that, as Dr Fuller says,[*]

> *'This tree delighteth in moist places and is triumphant in the Isle of Ely where the roots strengthen the banks and the top affords fuel for the fire. It groweth incredibly fast, it being a byword in this county that the profits by willows will buy the owner a horse before other trees will pay for his saddle.'*

In an older England, where, except in the stone counties, few buildings would be of stone and most would be walled in wattle and daub – fine for centuries if you keep the weather out – osier, willow and hazel were everywhere in building. Ely was one of the centres of a very ancient trade. Osiers, strong and whippy, made the best wicker: it was everywhere when I was a boy, in baskets that women took shopping, or you had on your bike handlebars – mine creaked and bent when you put heavy things in it – and in woven chairs that smelt deliciously woody. You saw sturdy wicker made into great baskets with two handles for carrying big loads, you saw it woven round

* Thomas Fuller, DD, *The History of the Worthies of England.* (1662)

glass bottles, even great carboys, to protect them from accidental knocks. It made dog beds, and cat baskets. It made elegant creels for fishing, that hung on your hip, and you hoped to fill them with trout and never quite did. Many of the sizes had remained standard for centuries, passed down from generation to generation – which is why we still talk about a 'cran' of herring (at least, I do...) and even fifty years ago the wicker baskets of Covent Garden porters' measures were sized on an ancient model. An Elizabethan laundry basket was big enough to take Falstaff and a load of laundry. From osier and willow countryfolk round here made grigs in which to trap the delicious eels, and wattles to fit between the studwork of walls to take the lime plaster. (Our house in Cow Lane has just such internal walls, as good as when the rods were cut in 1776.) As children at primary school we wove very thin wicker into baskets – they called it 'Handwork' – and centres for the elderly gave it to them to weave to help keep old hands supple. Wicker is one of the oldest means of making basketry and furniture in the world: it has been found in ancient tombs in the dry ground of Egypt, and the Roman poet Martial alludes in one poem to a wicker basket – he uses the Welsh word *bascuada* – that has got as far as Rome.[16] A kindly plant, of which one knows no ill. Like all the *salix* family, it also gives us the benison of aspirin.

Most osier or willow grown for basketry is a single year's growth. Commercially, the 'rod' men planted fields too wet to plough – there were many! – and cut the wands or whips in spring, before March, depending on the weather, when the fresh sap is beginning to make the bark loose and the almond-shaped leaves have not yet come. They cut close to the ground – though indeed I have seen willow and osier grown as a pollard – and each year many rods spring from the same place. I have an old osier knife, that came from Seth, a blade curved almost to a sickle shape, kept like a razor with a whetstone so that it would cut through a decent bunch, a bolt, of rods at a time. You always cut on a slant, pulling upwards, the bunch held against your body in the crook of the other elbow. Never cut directly across the rod; otherwise you make the work harder than it need be, and a day at it must in any case have been hard on the back. Never romanticise the past: it was damned hard work for most.

Then the wands had to be soaked, and were stood in water so that the bark would come off easily by pulling each stem through a piece of metal with a v-shaped slit fixed to something solid. Then they were then mellowed by further soaking, before the pliable golden stems could be made into beautiful and useful things. Women's work very often that was, that weaving of the smaller utensils. And well prepared wicker would last for years, and if it didn't, well, there was plenty more where that came from.

I have seen old photographs of boats piled high with the light cargo so that they looked like floating haystacks. They were taking the crop to where it could be prepared. I found just such a photo of a boat piled high with rods on Reach Lode, making its way to the lock at Upware, and then to Ely, for Ely was as Thomas Fuller says for many years a centre of the industry, and the market would have been full of the woven gold of new wicker. That load would have ended its journey, probably, at Fear's Rod Yard, near where Jubilee Gardens has now replaced with open green space and trees and a scented garden a sizeable part of the warren of small, smelly streets of densely packed terraced houses that once ran down to the river. Now the area between the city centre and the river is all tidied up and smart; but till the 1960s this is where the poor lived. Slums, some called them, and they were built out onto the flat, wet, soft ground, once fen, where the winter clamminess would creep up the walls. (But home, and warm in memory, to many.) And some street names, like Ship Lane – for ships were built in Ely – remember the old trades. Willow Walk, running down to the river, recalls just how important the osier and willow trade was.

A century or so ago, it was full of cut osier and willow rods at all stages of preparation and manufacture. Fear's Rod Yard had its own little cut off the river, just one of those little docks cut at right angles to the street at the foot of the hill down to the water, made over the centuries to increase wharfing space when the river buzzed with trade. (Some excavating of this ancient quarter was done in 2000.) It would be about here, on the hythe at the bottom of what it now Fore Hill, that the stone for the Cathedral would have been landed – good hard limestone from Barnack, Purbeck marble for decoration, and even the soft clunch from Reach, good for the rubble core of ashlar-faced walls, and for burning into the indispensable lime.

And let us not forget that this useful family of trees can be, simply, beautiful. And who can capture, even for oneself, in the sequential straitjacket of words, the sudden lift of the heart in the face of something beautiful, memorable?

It was the first mild, bright day in a wet and doolie March. I am taking the dog along the lane on the way to dunk him in the river. For one must at least attempt to get rid of the smell of the fox poo in which he has been luxuriously rolling, all four legs in the air. In that doggy ecstasy he is oblivious to any whistle. I am on the verge of grumpiness. But suddenly I walk into glory: a male goat willow in full flamboyant bloom, its golden stamens holding their yellow pollen clear of the main body of the flower so that you can see the sunlight as if in a mist through them. Next to it a blackthorn snowed with its white flowers promises the autumn bounty of sloes and the winter pleasure of sloe gin. The air is full of scent. When, decades ago, I used to smoke, I never noticed the subtle, delicate scents of such humble plants, but now I do, and suddenly the air is sweet. The bees – they might well be my neighbour's – have found the goat willow, and are busily fumbling the flowers. They are dusted all over with pollen, the yellow stripes on their abdomens almost grey with it. The tree will be pleased. And as they go about their work, the still air is full of the A-flat buzz of their wings. Touch the flowers and you have a thumb of gold. Touch, smell, sight, sound – all we need is taste for all senses to be satisfied, and we shall get that when Luke gives Rosanna and me a pot of the new honey. But the dog comes back impatiently, to see why I am standing still. Fox poo wins, and his bath calls. He loves swimming. A good thing.

Stone

Ely is short of good stone. When Tondberct prince of the Gyrwas (or Girvii, as Bede Latinises the name) settled the huge estate of over 600 hides* on Etheldreda when he married her in 652, his *villa regalis*, his Great Hall, would have been of wood, like Edwin of Northumbria's at Yeavering in Northumberland. I am pretty certain that that would have become the heart of the monastery for men and women she founded in 673. The monastic buildings the Danes burned in 870 were almost certainly wooden.

The City sits on a sandstone ridge buttered over by the clay the retreating glacier left behind. The ridge divides the Jurassic Kimmeridge clays from the Cretaceous limestones. It is a softish stone, which does not weather evenly or well, and is not a good building stone: it is inconsistent in hardness and hard to dress. Typically people used it in walling, individual blocks laid rough as general rubblestone held together by lime mortar. Around the old part of the town you can see dozens of old walls, or bits of old walls, made or part-made of it. It will stand long if you can keep the weather out, and its characteristic mellow brown colour delights the eye as you walk along the Gallery, especially near the Bishop's House and southwards towards Prior Walpole's great Porta, the new gatehouse to the monastery he built in the 1390s. Apart from that sandstone, the Isle has no stone worth speaking of. Occasionally in the Kimmeridge clay you do find harder concretions, but if

---

* A hide was enough land to support a peasant family. For perspective, Etheldreda's aunt, Hild, was given 61 by King Oswiu to found Whitby Abbey.

you tap them, as I used to when I was quarrying the clay for the coffer dam, they split. Useless for building. If you wanted to build anything elaborate, you need stones of reasonable consistency for load-bearing, and hardness to take the weather. Such stuff has to come from elsewhere. (You can see why the Brick Revolution of the fifteenth century – led from Holland, as was so much in this part of the world – was so welcomed.)

All stones have stories, and one of the joys of getting to know this new place has been trying to understand its old stones, trying to discover something of the men who hewed them, shaped them, carted them, hoisted them – and in some cases were crushed by them. Every single one has been handled by many hands roughed with work. The stone of Ely's big buildings came by water in flat bottomed barges… (Only after the railway network grew was it possible or economic to use the Ancaster limestone in any quantity.) Several, like the limestones, are relics of ancient life long before humankind was.

Once, I was repairing a garden wall at the house in Reach, and a large block of clunch fell to the ground and split into two halves. Where it split, perfectly preserved, was the fossil and burrow of a four inch long lugworm, exactly like the ones I use to dig up for bait when I was setting my nightline at low tide on the flat Lancashire coast of my youth. The two halves fit perfectly together. I carefully sawed them out of the larger block, and they have a prominent place in my Cabinet of Curiosities. That find was spectacular, and lucky. Then, decades ago, I split a piece of clunch and found in it a shell, like the little clam shells you pick up on the beach. I showed it to old Seth, who was standing by watching me make a mess of things as usual. 'That must have crawled into a crack and died,' he said. It was a surprise: but then, why should I have been surprised that he had no sense of geological time and the long past? It had never been part of his education or the culture in which he grew up. So I thought better of talking about the extinction of the dinosaurs – they had not then become that fashionable bit of natural history you can rely on most primary school children knowing, and the Jurassic had not yet had the attention of Hollywood.

Clunch is an interesting material, indeed. It almost beggars belief how, with the technology and labour force of the time, the vast quantities of stone needed for building even a simple chapel, let alone a great Cathedral, were quarried and transported. Quarry work is hard and dangerous, and sawing the stone a slow business – though clunch's softness, especially when wet from the face, yields easily to a saw's steel. But they did not have saws as we know them: hard sheet steel was not easily available till the 1200s, and the narrow strip blades of early saws had their teeth set so they cut on the pull stroke, and were set in a frame rather like a huge fretsaw. Our forebears did know how to make steel hard, though, and the teeth would bite in time even through granite. There were simple cranes, sometime powered by treadmill or horse gin, to lift the stone, and the yard on a cog – the workhorse vessel of the Middle Ages – could be swung round to act as a derrick for loading and unloading the blocks. And it worked: many consignments of the expensive creamy Jurassic limestone from Caen in Normandy came by water to Binham Priory in Norfolk, to Norwich Cathedral along the specially built canal from the Wensum, and the little river Tissey brought it to become part of the great Abbey at Wymondham.

Reach Hill, where all those years ago we villagers planted the trees that are now the wood, is a major post-industrial site, a quarry on the same scale as the quarries at Barnack – those 'Hills and Holes' are now a Nature Reserve. And active quarries do make a mess, however kindly nature tidies it up centuries later. The clunch quarried at Reach for over 1000 years was carried along the rivers and used all over Cambridgeshire, and a huge amount of it went into the building of the Norman Cathedral at Ely. This soft limestone will not stand weather well, but will bear load, and it can be burned for lime. It was dragged on sleds out of the quarry on the slow incline that was kinder to the straining horses, then slid along the deliberately wetted – wet clunch dust makes a mud as slippery as axle grease – track down to the dock which is still just visible in the garden of our old house. There the barge waited. Most of the walls and piers of the Cathedral have a filling of the stone that came from the hill behind the house, where at the edge of the new wood my last two dogs have bothered the rabbits and after many years the bee orchids the very old in the village remember from their childhood once more grow. And from nearby Burwell came a harder clunch, a Totternhoe limestone, which could be used for intricate carved work, as in the Lady Chapel at Ely Cathedral.

From the other side of the Fens came that hard limestone from Barnack, again along the water route: by sled – some blocks of stone were so big it needed sixteen oxen to drag them – to the river Welland, into barges, then down the Nene. Below Peterborough, the stone for Ely would have taken the route across the open water of Whittlesey Mere to Benwick and then along the West Water to Earith to join the Ouse to Ely. Up the Ouse (its channel was diverted to meet the sea at Lynn in 1236) came Purbeck stone, brought round the coast from Dorset. Those compressed fossils of millions of gastropods will take a high polish, and can gleam to look like a dark marble. It was much used in the high Middle Ages as a decorative addition to a building but it does not bear load well and its structure means that it is vulnerable to moisture. So those delicate colonettes in the Presbytery in Ely Cathedral are not doing the structural job they pretend, but are decorative. Of course, much of the white and cream glory of the newly created building would for centuries have been covered with paint. Our forebears had no taste – or, at least, not ours.

And the austere glory of the West Front, once symmetrical until the northwest tower collapsed,* would have had every niche filled with sculpted figures painted in high colour: the effect would have be stupendous, a gate of Heaven.

But why this huge labour and expense when Etheldreda and Aidan and Cuthbert could make do with wood, in all its grace? A thatched hut would keep the rain out. The cost of building a Cathedral, someone once calculated, was in terms of contemporary GDP far bigger than the entire NASA space programme of the last century, and had not even got the bad excuse of possible military use. The most articulate response to that dour,

---

* exact date unknown. Possibly about the same time as the central crossing.

killjoy puritan question was given near a millennium ago by Abbot Suger of St Denis (1081-1151):[17] through physical beauty the mind ascends to glimpse the beauty of God and Heaven, an uncreated light that we can only see through the limited lens of physical things, like sunlight streaming through windows that in many colours fracture it into stories, or like space divided up by stone and wood into pleasing shape and proportion. The act of building become an act of worship: and one reason why so much treasure was spent on the elaborate mathematical and proportional symbolism of buildings, on beautifying them with many different coloured stones, on paint, on the staining of glass, on elaborate metalwork, is that this effort might lead to a glimpse of the Heavenly Jerusalem built of precious stones described in St John's vision (Rev. 21:10ff.). Add music, and incense, and one can imagine how powerfully the building might affect the senses, and the vision – even if not primed by reading and teaching to be so moved. Buildings can do funny things to you: I once was asking a group of young folk who were about the leave The King's School what it was they would most remember about their time there. One of them said diffidently, as if he expected his peers to laugh, 'Well, going into the Cathedral every day.' Vigorous nods of agreement...

Why do we build such ugly, tawdry, badly built buildings to put our young folk, and ourselves, in? What are we doing? What does that say about how we think of them and ourselves? For physical environment does subtly influence how people mentally develop. Some things are of value beyond price.

The Reformation, necessary as it was, deliberately, and sometimes gratuitously meanly, destroyed much of beauty in this place and many of the destroyers, including the Crown, did very nicely out of it indeed. But you can see some point: destroy a monastic system that had been accumulating stone buildings good, bad, and indifferent for nearly 600 years, and you had an awful lot of spare space and capacity that was simply now redundant.

Some of it you could repurpose: the leper hospital chapel in what is now St John's Road became a farmhouse, for example. But there was an awful lot of useful stone tied up in redundant buildings in a town that had no stone of its own. So let them be quarries, without the bother of water transport: after all, Listed Buildings and English Heritage had not been invented yet. (I well remember, when I was very young, my naïve astonishment at seeing a Roman ('That's *Roman!*') altar from the Wall built into the crypt of St Wilfrid's church at Hexham, and my teacher told me that most of the older buildings in that part of the world were built of stone robbed from what was not then an Ancient Monument.) So everywhere you look in the old centre of the city you see old stone, some of it obviously worked, built into the walls of gardens, and houses. The House in Cow Lane leans its right elbow on that puzzling chunk of worked Barnack Rag. Quite a story, if walls could speak. They can't, so we have to guess.

Some stones are enduring puzzles. In the garden wall of Wellington House people every day pass a clearly re-used, weathered stone, which in its illegibility poses unanswerable questions. There was clearly once something like a face carved on it – or is it an urn? Just on a common or garden street... What is its story?

Saint and Protector

Spend any time in Ely and there are two people you can't avoid encountering. They are long dead, but they still resonate. Their lives, what they were, and what they did, indelibly marked the physical town we walk through, and the culture which we take for granted. It is only a courtesy we would desire for ourselves from our own successors to tip one's hat to them.

One is a saint – what does that mean? – and the other certainly not. Both are every bit as unknowably complicated and contradictory as everyone else, and it so easy to label them, and slip into thinking of them almost in caricature of the many coloured reality they were. (Don't we do that with the living as well as the dead?)

She needed translation: try saying Æþelþryð quickly – and anyway I always get all those Angles and

Saxons with names beginning 'Æþel' hopelessly mixed up. Latinising makes it much less of a tongue twister: Etheldreda. Common English tongues in time slurred that Latin smoothing of her Saxon name yet further, so by the twelfth century, when Marie de France writes her life, she has become St Audrey. (And then further corrupted to 'tawdry'...) As it happens, her name in Old English means 'Noble Strength', wholly appropriate for a woman who must have been a tough customer, who knew how to kick people's backsides to get her way. But how can we now get any idea of the sheer otherness of the life, mindset and times – and career – of this remarkable woman?

She lived in a very, very different world and with a very different way of seeing things, literally as well as figuratively. Even the plants and animals and foods we take for granted were different: no weeping willows before the 1700s, for example, or horse chestnuts before the 1600s; you would have never heard of tea, coffee, pasta, tomatoes, potatoes. You would soon have got fed up with the salmon which were so plentiful nobody wanted them, and the beavers in the river might have been a nuisance. And even if we know masses of facts, we can never really communicate or feel what living in those times was actually like. That world of the extraordinary sixth and seventh centuries will always be remote, another country. But without her *mariage blanc* at about 16 to Tondberct, who controlled the southern Fenland, which her father Anna, King of the East Angles, arranged to cover his western flank against the aggressive power of Mercia, she would never have been given the whole of the rich Isle of Ely as her own. She would never have founded what became one of the richest and most powerful religious houses in England. Her successors as Abbesses, later Abbots, later still Bishops, in this place would never have inherited from her the enormous, almost royal, power they wielded until the 1830s. Without her founding that wooden monastery (like many of the Irish and Northumbrian houses, for men and women) in 673, none of that would have happened, and the magnificence of the Cathedral buildings would not even have been a dream. Without her having been revered as a saint from only a few years after her death, the enormous wealth that the deplorable Henry VIII confiscated from the shrine he destroyed at the Dissolution of the monastery in the 1530s would never have gathered from the offering of the thousands of pilgrims, rich, poor, healthy, dying, who came here for 900 years.[18] In my short book about her, trying to think about what her world was like and how she ticked, left me with more questions than when I started. We don't even know where in Ely her monastery actually was, except that it was not where the Cathedral now stands. If her original monastery was adapted from the *villa regalis*, the rich wooden hall and buildings, of the property Tondberct had given her, we do not know where that was either. The burials, pretty well contemporary with the first generation of her monastery, which were recently excavated before They covered a lot of what was West Fen Farm with a whole lot of new houses, suggests the monastery cannot have been far away from there.

The finds from that dig eventually were exhibited in the Museum that was the old Ely gaol – the gaol in which men like the condemned Littleport Rioters, whom we shall meet later, spent their last night in this life. In the most important and richest of the burials, which had been covered by a barrow, lay the skeleton of a Christian woman clearly of high rank, who died at about the age of Elthedreda when she was married to Tondberct. I wondered what her story was... was she an example of that aristocratic and royal practice of sending, or parking, surplus daughters in a monastery until, like Etheldreda, you needed them for diplomatic marriage? Had that hand, when it was warm flesh, been taken by the saint, or her sister Sæxburh who followed her as Abbess?

For three queens were the first abbesses: Etheldredra (who in a second political *mariage blanc* married the 15 year old Ecgfrith of Northumbria), Sæxburh her sister, former queen of Kent, and Sæxburh's daughter, Ermenhild, widow of Wulfhere of Mercia. In so many places you see the arms (gules, three crowns or) which the Abbey adopted when heraldry as we know it became fashionable. They insist on its royal inheritance, and the Diocese that succeeded it still uses them. Everywhere you look a thread leads you back into the unknowable past, inhabited by people like us, but whose world circled a different sun...

When you have written a book, however elementary, about a person or a place, you feel that, somehow, you are no longer a stranger, but, well, that you belong. We humans need to belong...

And then there is Cromwell...

East Anglian Breweries, defunct since 1961, once brewed a beer called Old Noll in his honour. I can just remember seeing bottles of it. Then as now you can't be long in Ely without stubbing your toes on the memory of the late Oliver. I met an old chap only yesterday – he beats on the Reach shoot, and we were sharing our lunch sandwiches – and we were grumbling about the state of politics in this country, as one does, and he said, 'What we need is someone like that chap from Huntingdon. He sorted Parliament out. You know, farmed near Huntingdon, a few years back: he wouldn't stand for it. He'd kick their backsides.' Puzzled, I said, 'Do you mean Cromwell?' 'Yes, that's the chap. Couldn't get his name.' 'Course, it's sometime ago now, but that's what we need.' I wonder if the late Oliver would be pleased at how his memory endures?

In April 2022 *Country Life* ran a story headlined 'OLIVER CROMWELL'S FORMER LOCAL PUB COMES UP FOR SALE.' To be sure, the pleasant house down by the river which they mean was once an inn – the Three Crowns, perhaps inevitably. But the idea of the Lord Protector, even before he became so exalted, having a 'local pub' is not only anachronistic but downright bizarre. Yet the connection of the Cromwell family with this part of the world is real enough. Wily Thomas, Henry VIII's nearly all-powerful minister, was a distant relative, directly responsible for the dissolution of this Monastery – and Ramsey, and Crowland, and so on and so on – and the stripping of its assets: only the fact that the church had become a Cathedral in 1109 saved it from the fate of Rievaulx, and Fountains, and Glastonbury and so many others, bare ruined choirs where late the sweet byrd sang.

Oliver's connection is more direct than Thomas's. His family were smallish gentry in Huntingdonshire, within the same social orbit of the Montagu family at Hinchinbrooke as Samuel Pepys' people, but Oliver fell on hard times in the late 1620s: not only grave financial trouble, so that he was making only a yeoman's living by selling eggs and wool from the few hens and sheep he could keep, but he also suffered something like a mental breakdown, as we would say. It would have been diagnosed at the time as *melancholia adusta.* So difficult was this period that he sought to emigrate to Connecticut (if only!) where the Rule of the Saints on Earth might be thought to have begun. For this period also coincided with a profound religious conversion, which would have made him see the reforms – music, reverence, ceremonial – in the Church of England begun by Charles I's Archbishop Laud as downright Popery. Which they were not.

By the churchyard of the parish church of St Mary, which has the only peal (nine) of bells (modern) in the city, is a rambling half-timbered house. Bits of it were built when King John (an unattractive but somewhat maligned monarch) was having all that trouble with his barons. Reeds from the fen stiffen the daub between the timbers: serviceable building material if you keep the weather out with regular washings of limewash. After 1905 it came to serve as St Mary's Vicarage, but it was built as the tithe house for the Monastery – after the Reformation, for the Dean and Chapter. Here lived the farmer of the tithes, responsible for collecting the dues, which were often paid in kind – which is why huge tithe barns, like the one just inside the Porta which The King's School uses, were necessary in many great Church estates – and taking his cut for his work. By the 1600s it had become customary for son to follow father in the job. But the last farmer, Sir Thomas Steward, a person of some consequence, had no son to carry on the family tradition, and so his job passed to his daughter's son, Oliver Cromwell. He and his family lived in the house for some ten years, a time during which his fortunes began to mend. Spectacularly. His two youngest children (of nine) were born there – a sign, possibly, that his marriage to Elizabeth Bourchier was healing, for while there had been a child every two years in the early years, there was a 5 year gap before the births of Mary and Frances. Frances was baptised in St Mary's in December 1638, and lived until 1720, having made two aristocratic marriages, and, so say some with an inclination to gossip, having been of some interest to the future Charles II when her father was Lord Protector.

Cromwell's rise, and his membership of Parliament, led to appointment as Governor of the Isle of Ely in 1643. As everyone knows, he was no friend to the Established Church, and if all the legends of his stabling his horses in choirstalls were to be true, he certainly got around a bit with an extraordinary number of horses. As Governor, living in that house, he might have had Bishop Wren* as neighbour a hundred yards away at the palace Bishop Alcock had built. But Parliament in its wisdom had sent the good bishop to the Tower in 1642 for his efforts to retain some reverent ceremonial in public worship. So, for a time, William Hitch, the vicar of Holy Trinity parish, for which the erstwhile Lady Chapel had been made the parish church, was in charge.

Cromwell was a cultured man. When King Charles's art collection, perhaps the finest in Europe, was put up for sale by Parliament, Cromwell held back Mantegna's nine

---

* Matthew Wren was Christopher Wren's uncle. His brother was Dean of Windsor, and had to flee with his young family when the Deanery at Windsor was attacked.

huge paintings of the Triumph of Caesar, still at Hampton Court, and the Raphael cartoons of the Apostles (now in the Victoria and Albert Museum). There are, I think, interesting ideological reasons for his doing that: after all, he had crossed his own Rubicon. He was also, like the king whose death warrant he had signed, passionately fond of music, and masque, that elaborate precursor of opera, and had an organ installed at Hampton Court when he was Lord Protector. Ironically, it was the one that was ordered to be removed from the chapel of Magdalen College, Oxford. He had the best of musicians in his pay, to solace him in relaxation from cares of state – there were very many – and to teach his daughters. When his daughter Frances married, they had '48 violins and much mirth with frolics, besides mixt dancing.' Like many Puritans, he had no objection to music or singing outside the church services, but anything remotely 'Popish', and a church service with a choir was so classed, as 'unedifying and offensive'. On January 10, 1644, Cromwell wrote to William Hitch:

> *Mr Hitch,*
> *Least the soldiers should in any tumultuarie or disorderly way attempt the Reformation of your Cathedral Church, I require you to forebear altogether your choir services, so unedifying and offensive – and this as you shall answer for it if any disorder should arise thereupon. I advise you to catechise and read and expound the Scriptures to the people; not doubting but the Parliament with the advice of the Assembly of Divines will direct you further. I desire your sermons too where they usually have been, but more frequent. Your loving friend, Oliver Cromwell*

Hitch ignored this shot across his bows. Cromwell, his hat on (in those days deeply insulting), marched into the Cathedral in the middle of a service and, sword drawn, brusquely said to Hitch, 'I am a man under authority and am commanded to dismiss this assembly. Leave off this fooling and come down.' Hitch continued saying the prayers at the communion table, not only ignoring Cromwell's interruption, but the fact that the Governor was followed by 40 soldiers armed with swords and guns, and followed by the usual rabble of disaffected people looking to enjoy a bit of trouble.

Cromwell had his way: and the vaulting of the Cathedral, which a century before had resounded to the music of Christopher Tye, lay clerk and then choirmaster through all the tempests of the reigns of Henry, Edward, Mary and Elizabeth, fell silent... Until England at last woke herself from the long nightmare of war and military rule and the bitter divisions where neighbour informed on neighbour, and old friendships and families were riven asunder by ideology. Cromwell did not wish that: poor man, like all who seek power, he was trapped into a web of events he could not control, and could only walk backwards into the future, patching here, mending there, with no clear plan.

Every time I walk past that house, with its lifesize effigies of man and woman in the seventeenth century dress befitting people of moderate substance, I can't help remembering the might-have-beens: the Civil War was not inevitable. It was not written in the unceasing stars that Oliver had to 'ruin the great work of Time/And cast the Kingdom old/ Into another Mold,' as John Milton's successor as Latin Secretary, the poet Andrew Marvell, put it; the pain and travail it caused the people caught up in its consequences need not have happened; the long division in English society that persists to this day as the fallout (with a long half-life) of that War might have been avoided. And, worst of all, none of the actors in that great drama of state were villains – though they allowed villains to flourish. Poor Oliver. Do the tourists who flock to the house ever catch a ghost of Frances' infant chatter, or the scratch of Oliver's pen as he writes that letter to Mr Hitch?

As it happens, some five years after poor Fitch's being bullied, an order was made in the Commons that 'the Cathedral Church in the Isle of Ely, being in a ruinous condition, should be examined with a view to its being pulled down and its material used to make provision for sick maimed soldiers and their families.' Parliament was, indeed, broke: sounds familiar? But probably it was decided it would cost more to pull down the Cathedral than could be raised by the sale of the materials.

One searingly hot and airless Sunday in June, we were in Ely Place, off Holborn, where stood until the 1530s the grand London residence of the Bishops of Ely. It is a peculiar:[19] with its gated boundaries it was for centuries subject to the jurisdiction ecclesiastical and secular not of the Crown or the London magistrates but of the Bishop as Etheldreda's successor as Prince of the Isle of

Ely. Vestiges of that jurisdiction endured into the 1960s, when the tiny pub, the Mitre, was still licensed by the Cambridgeshire magistrates and not those of London. (Reputedly, Elizabeth I, who loved dancing, and her favourite partner, the glamorous commoner she knighted and made Lord Chancellor, Christopher Hatton, danced round the cherry tree against which the front leans.) In the 1350th year after Etheldreda founded her monastery, I had been invited to speak at the patronal festival of the church of St Etheldreda, which was built in the 1320s by good Bishop Hotham of Ely as the private chapel of his London residence. High Mass over, friendly (and generous) drinks followed in the little garden under an ancient fig tree and red umbrellas – necessary in that hot sun, if not exactly creating *la vie en rose* – advertising quite decent champagne.

Then, over a very good lunch afterwards in the crypt, more talk flowed, as it does, new connections were made, new discussions started, and the afternoon wore on... We got to talking about relics, and how I had seen once the fully accreditable relic of St Boniface – his hyoid bone – which King Offa of Mercia had given to the great church at Brixworth in Northamptonshire in the 780s. We talked about the pillaging of Etheldreda's shrine, and the cruel scattering of her body to the four winds, and how one of her hands had somehow been squirrelled away, to turn up again, with a credible provenance, in the 1820s. Most of it is enshrined in the RC church in Egremont Street in Ely. But part of the palm is in Ely Place, and Father Tom offered to display it to a few of us. So, into the church, empty save for the angels… Something of the morning's incense was still in the air. A wait, and then Fr

Tom returned, reverently holding the reliquary, a silver hand with a crystal let into the palm to reveal the relic. It was an odd moment: curiosity, certainly; awe, yes, at its age, and how it connects 'now' with a very different 'then' and puts both in a perspective that is unsettling. And, yes, reverence. I felt called to say to the others, 'Well, I hope I have not let her down in the book.' Inadequate. My mediaeval ancestors would have been on their knees. As Fr Tom left us to replace the relic in its secret place, Michael the warden said to me, 'I am not very sure how I feel about relics.' Indeed: how does a 21st century person relate to that culture that for us was so rudely terminated, on some grounds which were arguably sound, at the English Reformation?

Tawdry is as Tawdry Does

If you want a solely religious life, you had probably better find a convenient wilderness where the ravens will deliver your meals at regular times: as they did to the prophet Elijah. For as soon as you live in a community, however devoutly religious it may be, you get involved in economics. Big monasteries, like Ely or Bury St Edmunds in our part of the world, could not be just quiet places of prayer and patient copying and reading of books. They had to be self-supporting day to day, and that means work – often noisy, smelly, grubby work in field or foundry or building site. Indeed, the Benedictine Rule explicitly says that monks must engage in physical work each day, and there was so much to do that they could not help becoming major employers of lay labour as well. At one time, indeed, they *owned* it, for they had their serfs and, in the manors they were given, their villeins who were tied to the land. So, just like the Roman forts of centuries before, outside their gates there often grew up a settlement for these folk, which became a village, which became a small town, and that small town needed its own economic support in trades and services and market. Today, as I walk round the centres of Bury or Ely, I can often ignore the dull fronts of modern shops and the strident displays of and adverts for things I neither need nor want, and be aware of the generations before me who followed the layout of the streets of the grid on which a thousand years ago such settlements grew. Planning is not a new thing.

Building and maintaining a big church building is expensive. Feeding and clothing a community – even in the rough wool of a monastic habit – is expensive. Providing the support for the poor, in handouts of food, and clothing, and for the aged and sick in hospitals, is expensive. Doing something about maintaining the roads, and building bridges over the rivers – after all, the Latin word for priest, *pontifex,* does mean 'bridge builder'! – is expensive. Put all these things together – and there are more – and you have a pretty constant demand for money, and you can't always rely on handouts and benefactions from your rich friends. You have got to generate your own income.

One of the most useful things a lord, lay or ecclesiastical, possessed, apart from property, was the right to hold a regular market. There was an income from the dues payable by the traders, for example. But if you could win from the Crown (the final source of all ownership, and law) a right to hold a major fair as well, even better. A fair was a special occasion, to which many people with money to spend would come from far away to buy the necessities that were not daily ones, but special, needed perhaps once or twice a year, or things you might buy in bulk to sell on piecemeal at a profit. Such fairs could draw people from beyond the seas, indeed, and, in their heyday, at Cambridge's Stourbridge or Frankfurt or at Troyes in Champagne, you would have heard just about every European language as well as Arabic.

Ely's great fair has now almost slipped out of memory. In 1189, Henry II, that energetic and hot-tempered prince – when as a mildly careless child I read about him I always misread 'Angevin' as 'Angrevin', for I had heard that he would roll around on the ground in his paroxysms of anger – granted the Abbot and Monastery the right to hold a fair each year in honour of Saint Etheldreda. It lasted a full week, culminating on the anniversary of the translation of her relics to the Abbey Church on 17 October. Granting a charter – in effect permission – for a fair was a royal prerogative, and Henry did this probably not out of special generosity or devotion, but in return for a consideration, as the Crown has never not been strapped for cash.

From the Abbey's point of view, it was worth whatever they came up with: markets were a very good investment, for they generated revenue for the owner of the right of market, who could charge stallholders market dues, and also had the right to hold a court of pie powder (*Pieds poudreux*, 'dusty feet' – from travelling), and to the proceeds of any fines there imposed. These annual fairs often grew into really big things, with some having international importance: Frankfurt's survives as the annual Book Fair where literary agents and publishers try to sell rights to books like this; Cambridge's Stourbridge Fair in September, once one of the largest in Europe, survives now only as a funfair; at the great fairs, in July and November, of Troyes in Champagne, weights and measures were so trusted that we still talk about Troy Weight. Sometimes they specialised: Stourbridge was especially a cloth fair; Reach's Rogationtide fair, granted to the Mayor and Burgesses of Cambridge by King John, later specialised in unbroken Welsh ponies and other horseflesh – but of course they also attracted a range of sellers from all around, from the mixed contents of the usual pedlar's pack to fast food stalls, and also ladies of questionable reputation, pickpockets, hucksters, quacks, toothdrawers and mountebanks making money from fast talk and selling people dreams. It was also a good place for more solid citizens to meet people and make pacts and bargains. Ely's Fair was noted for fabrics and lace, and one speciality was lace collars. St Etheldreda died from a tumour on her neck – it was possibly a quinsy – and was a helper saint in throat and neck complaints: hence the 'tawdry' collars sold at her fair.* But the lace collars were certainly not all rubbish, and the word does not seem to have a pejorative sense in 1548, when *OED* first records it.

Those big fairs were a grand chance to meet people from further away than your usual orbit, and to stock up on things that are not normally available. But, as

---

* They had often been 'touched' against her shrine and so were eagerly bought by pilgrims. Until about 1913, according to Enid Porter's *Cambridgeshire Customs and Folklore*, pieces of lace called St Audrey's Chains were sold at Ely Fair.

well, weekly markets for food, clothing and all the other essentials grew up all over Europe, usually spaced so that within, say, ten miles – the distance a man can walk there and back in a day – you can get the goods and services you need. Ely, like Bury, Cambridge, the NewMarket (that used to be at Exning until they moved it sometime in the 12th century)* and hosts of other places all had weekly or even daily markets. Suppose you had been living in one of the villages. Well, on a market day you could walk into one of those towns, you could buy clothing, tools, produce, leather goods, pottery and so on, and also exchange gossip, do business of substance, and if young and foolish perhaps do a bit of courting, or whatever. The many trades and services of a small market town made it pretty well self-sufficient.

The Corn Exchange in Bury St Edmunds, or Cambridge or in Ely's Market Place, or countless other towns in the arable counties of England was an (self)important building befitting the solemnity of the bargains made there. But the market town was a place for pleasure too, where besides the amusements for the many, the solider farmers, people in the professions, and the local gentry, would gather in the winter months for balls. (Which gave employment to musicians.) Your daughter might find a husband there to take her off your hands, or your son a suitable match – after all, marriage was often as much (or more) to do with property as with love.[20] You might go to a bank if you were one of those lucky ones who had a bank account – after banks were invented. (Even recently, not all folk used them: when old

---

* The suggestion of Thomas Dibdin, Vicar of Exning 1823-47, that it was moved because of an outbreak of plague is not now generally accepted.

Tom Cooper died in a nearby village I know well in 1968 – he had locked up his shop, and its stock, twenty years earlier and never turned the key again – they found his mattress stuffed with the old white £5 notes which even then were no longer legal tender.) On Ely High Street, there is a deeply carved bit of sandstone hardly noticeable over a dull modern shop front: that was the London and County Bank, founded 1836, once the largest bank in the country: it became the nucleus of NatWest. It reminds me of a time when bank managers tried to stop you getting into debt and were very cross when you did. (I do remember, indeed…) You might need to see a lawyer about that bit of land you wanted to buy or sell: Archer and Archer were there in the building on the Market Square where they have been for generations. One could go on…

I love markets – proper markets. I remember Kendal when I was a boy, and loved going there with my (honorary) uncle and aunt. I love pottering through a French market, like my favourite in Paris, in the gardens that now cover the Canal de St Vincent, with its mouth-watering and odorous food stalls. Not so long ago, we used to go regularly to Bury St Edmunds on a Wednesday: the pubs were open all day, everything you could want to buy was on sale, people were in holiday mood, the cattle and poultry market was in full swing – many times I bought my ducks and geese and hens there, and then had to get them home despite their noisy protests. From the village up to the 1970s the local bus service ran a Special every Wednesday to Bury, and it was always packed. Their buses had an advert on their sides advertising not a shop or new film but, sensibly, poultry food: 'Ray-o-Vitol', with a picture of an erupting volcano. Farmers round here kept a polished pair of Wellingtons for going to market. Women wore hats.

Bury's cattle market is now gone to car parking and shops, just as Ely's is under the Waitrose supermarket. I miss them. But I love Ely's market, just wandering around gawping at the beauty of the vegetable stalls and the shapely beauty of the fish on the fishmonger's, or just sitting watching, (over)hearing people's voices, and I think, 'This is not a bad place to be.' Sometimes a phrase or sentence, heard out of context, keeps me happily puzzled for a morning: 'And this, my dear, is where I were poisoned...'; 'you just put that cider back and get back in your pushchair...'; '...I got 'er all nicely tied up...'

Sometimes I go to the quiet early morning Eucharist in the Cathedral and come out just as the market is setting up. Breakfast can wait – anyway, if I want it, I can get a good coffee on the market square. Dogs and their walkers dot the Green, and run delightedly up and down the grassy slope of the old Norman motte chasing balls their owners have thrown. Joggers importantly run past, intent on their feet and their headphones, in bright Lycra to frighten off the traffic. They never look as if they are enjoying themselves. I am more sober in port and demeanour, and enjoy the feast of the senses that walking down the High Street to the market gives me. Leaving the Cathedral precincts through the 16th century Steeple Gate is always a delight: the two worlds of Ely joined by a division, and I am reminded of how this gate was the laity's entry to the precincts of the monastery, where they could only go on sufferance.[21] Almost opposite is the window of the excellent Topping's bookshop, with sometimes one of my new books displayed – always gratifying! Look up above the mostly modern shop fronts, and the ages of the buildings can easily be read – and there is the delight of a lovely oriel window. (Is it Regency? It is always such a mistake not to stop and look up when walking down an old street in an old town. The anonymity of modern shops can suddenly acquire interest.) By the little lane that leads off to Butchers' Row the Romanian lady, for whom Rosanna always buys a coffee and a croissant, is settling down to another day selling *The Big Issue*, a magazine whose principles are impeccable and whose material is more interesting – and better written – than that of most glossier publications. The market on the square is for me the greatest of timewasters, when I should be getting back to writing and getting ready for lecturing. Bric à brac – well, yes, but we have enough already and my heirs will probably be able to open a stall.

But antique tools, there is the temptation. Whose hands wore and polished these moulding planes? The very touch of them connects you to the men – yes, men, for good tools, perfect in form for their job, were passed down from father to son, from master to apprentice – who made beautiful things with them. Where did this horse gag come from? It must have been a big animal, and I hope it did not mind its drench. Or who last used this bull ringer? That is a saw set just like the one Seth gave me, which I now hardly use. Rosanna says my sheds could stock his stall, but he is not having any yet. Hours could, do, pass… the Fishmonger has arrived, a feast of delight for eye – I think fish some of the most beautiful creatures on our planet – and nose. The stall is far, far more hygienic than the stalls that the ancestors would have known – indeed, that I knew as a boy, when cheap reliable and portable refrigeration was non-existent.* The Cheese and Pie Man tempts. And is sometimes successful, if Rosanna is not looking. Flowers and plants, gungy cakes, Indian and Polish street food – it's all there. And at the corner, where the road does a steep dive down Fore Hill to the river, is the biggest time-consumer of all, the bookstall. He never interrupts my browsing, knowing I might well buy. But where will I put yet another book?

Rosanna shares my enthusiasms, here as in so many other things. Whenever we are in Ely she goes on market day to scan the stalls, buys lots of the veg I don't grow and dourly say we probably don't need (but still enjoy), talks to lots of people, and comes home thoroughly happy. But any sort of shopping, even in markets I like, is for me a pleasure that soon wears thin with use.

Talking of which... coming out of Toppings bookshop, having descended its no-nonsense, noisy, uncarpeted stairs from its second floor with more circumspection than once would have been the case, I bump into Bernard. He is just about to go in to see what is new, and to read a few pages before he buys – as I do – to see if the reviewers had actually read the book. (I had just picked up and read a chapter of a wildly hyped book, and found it shallow and nearly unreadable.) But, of course, we stop, and talk, oblivious of the people who want to go into the shop or pass on the pavement. They must get annoyed with these

---

* Even the deep-water trawlers on which I worked for a time had no refrigeration, only a hold full of ice, slowly melting. Some 'fresh' fish sold at the wholesale auction in Fleetwood had been dead and in melting ice for three weeks.

two white beards wagging away as if they had all the time in the world. (We don't.) We demolish some of last week's contributors to the *Times Literary Supplement* and *London Review of Books*. We know we could have done a better job. Bernard asks me if I had noticed how X, whom we both know, in criticising a certain book's style, had committed several grammatical howlers himself. We nod sagely, sadly. But then it is time to part: he that way, me this. I have come away empty handed, which is a sort of triumph. He said, wearily, 'She says I must not get any more books, but I know I shall.' I know exactly what he means, and then they glare at you from the pile of 'To Be Read', as if saying silently, 'Read Me! Read Me!'

But in this peregrination something is missing. The Kendal I knew when we went to market all those years ago smelt. If the wind was southwest, you could smell the reek of the tannery for K Shoes a mile or so downwind. If in the north west, you got the strong, not unpleasant odour of Gawith's snuff mill in Lowther Street. Snuff has been made in Kendal since 1782. The famous Kendal Brown, still made, is flavoured with camphor. (On the wall of the shop is an effigy of a Saracen or Turk, smoking a long-stemmed pipe and holding a roll of tobacco.) In still weather the smell of coal from people's fires lingered. Just so in the Fleetwood I knew as a boy: the iodine smell of the mudflats of the Wyre at low tide, the wonderful smell of kippers being smoked in the smokery on Dock Street, the pervasive smell of fish near the docks where the trawlers came in. Their fish was sold by auction to dealers in trilby hats who sent it off in clanking railway wagons through the inland shires of England to the grand smelling fish and chip shops of the big industrial towns. (If unluckily the wind was southeast, Fleetwood got the acid whiff of the ICI chemical works a couple of miles upstream.) Bury on market day was a torrent of smells: cattle stale where the wagons had drained while waiting for the traffic lights to change, fish and chips, flowers, cheap scent when you brushed up again women in the crowd in the pubs, beer...

Ely for centuries, and up to a few decades ago, must have had a smellscape at least as varied, but I never knew it fully so. I can recall the sickly, sweet smell of the sugar beet factory out near Queen Adelaide: from the dried pulp they made pony nuts that we used to give to the ponies, and I know my ever-hungry young daughter secretly ate them, tempted by their sweetness.

I can recall the two breweries;[22] Entwistle's tannery and leather factory faced the East Anglian Brewery (they who made the beer called 'Old Noll', in homage to Cromwell) at the bottom of Fore Hill, and down by the river was the maltings for Harlock's Brewery – and once upon a time there was a monastic brewery near the Porta, the gateway to the monastery precincts, for everyone from beggar's brat to bishop drank beer. A limekiln down by the river smoked. The gasworks in Potter's Lane emitted the usual throat-catching smell typical of that industry, now forgotten by all except people of my age – I would not wish it back; the jam factory filled the air with sugary sweetness; the cattle market on its due days brought the smell of cowpat and pigsty, and in the heart of the town, Butchers' Row with the smell of blood and offal and all the meat smells a dog could want. It must have been, as for most country towns, a rich symphony of smells. And that is all before we imagine a time before sewers, when the cesspits had to be dug out by the night soil men and the mature manure spread on field and garden.

The prevailing wind is westerly in this quarter of the globe. No wonder the classier folks, when they could afford it, built their homes on the west side of towns, and the poor stuck it out in the East End. As they did in Ely, where slums fringed the river. Now expensive houses and a park have taken their place.

Mentioning sugar beet brings back some powerful memories: how our hens used to love having a few in their pen to peck at, and how Robbie, best loved of all the ponies that kept our daughter more or less too tired for mischief loved the raw roots I would snaffle for him from the heap waiting by the road for the lorry to take it to Ely. It was a filthy crop to lift, mud was everywhere, all over the roads, and vehicles, and as the winter wore on the waiting heaps began to smell of rot, and, in the really old days before the clever mechanisation came in, it was a crop that had to be singled when it was young, and each root trimmed by hand when it was time to lift it as autumn drew on into winter.

I can just remember lines of women with hoes working across a field, gapping the rows so each plant had room to grow. During the winter 'campaign' (as they called it) of getting in and then processing the sugar beet, from the Sugar Beet factory rose constant clouds of sweet smelling steam, seen and smelt miles away downwind across on the flat fen. Along the roads to Ely came a constant stream of lorries – much smaller then, 3 tonners mostly – full of the crop. Earlier, before WWII when the concrete roads were laid in the Fens by the War Agricultural Committees, you simply could not move a loaded cart in winter weather along the soft droves of the fens: water transport was essential. So even now, dotted all over the fen, you will find little hythes, with slades leading up to them, where the 40 foot lighters could be loaded. At the factory they would queue up sometimes four abreast to be emptied and sent back for more. But the first job was to wash the soil off the roots, and 'believe me, that old fen dirt, 'er do cling on'.

This presented a problem: the water from the river could do the washing, but what do you do with the dirty water? It was piped across the river and discharged into a series of settling ponds, and when each was silted full, the next one was used. But now there was all that soil to be got rid of...

On Jam and Marmalade, and Other Things

Food and memory… For Proust it was a madeleine. For me, an old advert for sale on Ebay, seen by pure chance: 'St Martin CHUNKY Marmalade. With all its delicious flavour and pre-war quality'. (Is not the 'pre-war' revealing?) We had that marmalade on the table at home when I was a lad – in the late 1940s, in fact, the date of the advert. We bought it from the little shop at the end of our road in the big village where I grew up. I liked it – it was a lot better than the tinned 'Koo' marmalade from South Africa I also remember from the '40s. I had a habit of reading everything, even labels, as a child and I can recall now, word perfect, the French side of the label of the HP Sauce Harold

Wilson was reputed to love. The Chunky Marmalade label, I remember, said that the company that made it had factories in Maidenhead, Newcastle and Ely. And here I am writing about, and in, Ely: you have only to go back a few decades and you find a town that was noted for the fine jam made at St Martin's Jam Factory at the end of Bray's Lane. For the edge of the Fen and the Isle were important soft fruit growing areas, feeding the Ely factory and the Chivers factory in Histon. One week it would be the smell of the boiling of strawberries or raspberries from Willingham that sweetened the wind that breathed over north Cambridge, another time it would be blackcurrants, another plums. Indeed, many named varieties were bred in the area... How rapidly things we thought would always be there are forgotten – a single generation is enough. Who now remembers the iron foundry in Thompsons Lane in Cambridge – in the garden I have a cast iron lavatory cistern, 'The Cambridge', which they made – or the gas works in Potter's Lane in Ely, or the Fleetwood Ribble bus depot where a youth that was me once worked as a conductor?

Late July, and the beginning of school holidays and the easy season... The many, many orchards that once were so common in the Isle would be long past the glory of their spring blossom. When the foam of blossom had washed up the steep south slope up to Haddenham and Wilburton, people looked anxiously for signs of a killing frost. If the afternoon sky was clear and a little mean wind had set in the north or east, they might put bales of straw at the windward end of the rows of trees, and set match to them to smoulder through the night and let the wind carry the slightly warmer air and smoke through the orchard. But by late July the leaves were beginning to look tired, and if all had gone well the fruit was set and full, and blushing to ripeness.

First fruit to appear on the market stalls in Ely and Cambridge and Bury were the small purple czar plums, deliciously sweet and sharp at the same time, with a bloom on them a finger's touch could rub off, and a scent all their own. This was the signal for us to get ready for the yearly chore, and pleasure, of bottling fruit. Hardly anyone had freezers then, and you bottled fruit, sterilising it in water in big Kilner jars in an oven warm enough to kill bacteria and cool enough not to stew the fruit. (We also salted down jar on jar of runner beans.)

Parentheses and asides will happen… never mind. Those Kilner jars had a story. On the top of the hill behind the village in an old clunch pit was the council dump. It was the sort of place any parent forbids children to play in, and which children equally instinctively love and seek out. And I can see why. Rubbish dumps are interesting long before they become archaeological, and quite apart from the pleasure in all the forbidden hideouts the place offered, there was treasure in what people had thrown away. My son Justin, aged eight, came back one day stooping under the weight of an old sack full of perfectly usable Kilner jars: we cleaned them, got new rings for them, and forty and more years later use them still. (Another time, when the smell from the hill had for a time been particularly ripe, he persuaded me to follow him up there to collect what he had found. Feeling my age, I followed his determined little back, and really rather agreed with him when he proudly showed me the luxuriant crop of tomatoes and marrows growing all along one side of the hill. For someone had dumped a load of sewage sludge there at exactly the right time. And others soon cottoned on: for the next few weeks everyone in the village had tomatoes.)

To return: we would set off, the two of us, on our bicycles, with big wicker baskets on our handlebars and tied to the carrier over the back wheel. No point in not doing it in good weather: so I remember perfect summer afternoons, with cauliflowers of cumulus gently and gravely punctuating the sky. First came the long ride down Little Fen Drove, past where the National Trust re-wilding land would later be. Sometimes near a roadside tree you would pass through a mist of insects, their tiny bodies brushing against your face and annoyingly getting into eyes. There the road left the more solid ground, the chalky marl, of the 'white' land, to cross the black soil of the deep fen, which flexed with a wet season and shrunk in a dry one. Then came the abrupt climb out of Below Sea Level – the drained fen gradually slopes down – up to the lock at the end of the coral limestone peninsula where sits Upware. On our right the lovely view up Reach Lode to where Wicken Lode joins it, and the cock-up bridge at the end of Wicken Fen nature reserve. Only pleasure boats now cruise that water, though there is one of no fixed abode that has a sack of coal and a bicycle on the roof and is home to someone.

A mile or so further on – the road running on the limestone feels different under the wheels from the roads over the fen, and the soil on each side is a rich tan colour – you join a bigger road. You pass the vast limestone quarry the dust of which can whiten the hedges for miles, and you come to the concrete bridge over the Cam where you can't see the river over the parapet. Once it was called the Military Bridge, for it was built in the early years of the 1914-18 war so that troops could be rushed to East Anglia to counter any German landing in Norfolk – as was indeed plausibly feared.[23] North of it the broad river passes a wetland, well below its own level, now a reserve of some 400 acres. There, now, the slow, thoughtful (I think…) water buffalo graze standing knee deep and still in the weed-covered water. The place is loud with calls of the declamatory geese (they put the emphasis on the first syllable…) and the harsh screech of blackheaded gulls. Then, off the bridge and dive down sharply into Mesopotamia, as I call it, that strange black land between the Cam and the Old West River, bisected by the Cambridge–Lynn railway. The peat echoes with the noise of the train passing over it and as you wait by the level crossing when the train passes you can feel the ground quivering. When it is hot the peat has a strange hot musty smell; if smells had colour, you would say it was dark brown. The quiet flag and rush fringed stream you glimpse as you cross the Old West River is all that is left of the mighty river that once overwhelmed the Cam, and rushed their mingled waters past the steep bluff of Stuntney. In winter flood it spread itself across the Fen to the hill where no stone Cathedral yet stood. But that was before the genius of Vermuyden and the capital of the Duke of Bedford emasculated its torrent and sent the waters of the Midland shires down the straight cuts of Old and New Bedford rivers.

Here the flat black land is now some of the most intensively cultivated in northern Europe. Heaven knows what chemicals are sprayed on it to grow weedless acres of this crop and that, sometimes twice a year. In summer's drouth clouds of dark brown dust dog the tractors. Once, that dust was the living growth of the ancient fen. In winter, when we are lucky, we have seen a host of whooper swans, just flown in from Iceland, to winter in a kinder climate, and hear – you must stop, and switch off the engine, and be still for a moment – their grave calls which make a music that sings of the spare lands of the far and lonely north I love.

Then came Stretham, the *ham* on the *straet*, the Roman road that leads to Ely and then on (perhaps, but nobody is sure how) to the coast and the first of the forts of the Saxon Shore that ringed the coast round to Portchester. It is a village we always liked, and used to stop for a pint at its welcoming pub, sometimes before, sometimes after, the last section of the ride to Wilburton. There the gentle lift of the land told you that you were truly on the Isle, and on each side orchards – plum, damson, greengage (if there had been no late frost), apples, pears – fringed the road. It is so hard not to regret the grubbing up of the old native varieties in so many well-cropping orchards and their replacement in our shops with dull, Identikit stuff brought in from abroad. Why, when England grows the best fruit in Europe? Is not Avalon, the land of heart's desire of the Celts, *Ynys Affalon*, 'the isle of apple trees'?

There was a farm we regularly went to each year – until the owner died, and the trees were grubbed up and burned. (What a waste!) Czars, a couple of stone, then a fortnight or so later, Pershores, and finally the richness of the 'Vics' (Victorias) and the greeny gold of greengages. It could be a sticky business on hands and face after initial tasting to see if they would do and then loading of the baskets. Few of the greengages ever got near the bottling. Getting home was always a slow business, companionably and unhurriedly cycling side by side – for the roads were much less busy than now, and you could do that for miles. The baskets were pretty full, and one had to go steadily, and one plum led to another, so that the baskets were less full, and on a warm afternoon a dawdle at the pub by the river at Upware called. And so home, and a kitchen that for days would be full of the smell of fruit raw, and fruit made into jam. It was cluttered with the sealed Kilner jars, or the jam jars of all shapes and sizes we had carefully washed and saved over the year for this first harvest of the year. We were only doing what almost everyone else was doing – though we were perhaps unusual in doing it on bikes.

One farmer in the Isle diversified, and put an acre over to vines: Müller-Thurgau, a favourite German wine grape – palatable, too, as a dessert. He once told me it was the most profitable bit of his farm, and he sold most of what he pressed to the French firm of Nicolas for blending into *vin de différents pays de la communauté Européenne*. Perfectly drinkable. A cutting of one of his vines came to me, and it grew for years along the front of the house in the village. It cropped: and came a year when I made what I hoped would be wine. It looked and smelt all right, and greatly daring I sent a bottle over with my son to a *viticulteur* friend in Beaujeu for whom he was going to work for a few months. Came the day when they decided to try it. Patrick sniffed it; rolled it round his *coupe*; tasted it; put his *coupe* down, and said to my son, 'Tell your father to eat his grapes next time.' But: Justin learned a lot about wine, not least that some raw wines need added sugar, and so next year I pressed another bumper crop, fermented it and added sugar and sugar and sugar until it begged for mercy. I bottled six bottles of a lovely golden aromatic fluid, and left it to do its own thing for several years. Came a dinner party, and a friend who prided himself on being something of a connoisseur of wine. I decided to risk the wine – I myself had not tasted it, though I knew it would be sweet – at the end of the meal when his guard might be a bit down. I decanted the clear liquid, and delicate sweetness filled the air. At dessert I placed it on the table, saying, deprecatingly, 'This may amuse you.' He lifted his glass. I too. The bouquet was fine. He sipped. I sipped: definitely OK. He sipped again, and set down his glass. 'Charles, this really is a very nice Sauternes. Thank you.'

I never owned up.

That vine liked Reach, had pups, and they clambered all over the stable I built, and the shed, and they have grapes, but never again like that year's. The blackbirds love them, and welcome. Meanwhile, two vines, a Chardonnay and a Sauvignon, are beginning tentatively to feel their way along the mellow walls of the House in Cow Lane. We are still in touch with the friend, and who knows...

This ramble began with a label from a pot of marmalade, and it will close with a compliment. As I remember from my childhood, around January the big, bitter Seville oranges begin to appear on the market stalls, and we buy them to make marmalade. I have to say that Rosanna makes the best marmalade I have ever had. Having married her I do not need St Martin Chunky, or Frank Cooper, or Tiptree, or Fortnum and Mason, for I have a talented (if sometimes sticky) wife. The difference between my childhood and now is that we can buy a lot of oranges and store them in the freezer: there were no freezers when I were a lad. That means that if later in the year I am burrowing for a frozen pheasant or something, and I come upon a bag of oranges, I can triumphantly extract them, and anticipate that soon there will be the ravishing smell all over the house of cooking marmalade. So the pleasure that once was seasonal can be repeated. An improvement.

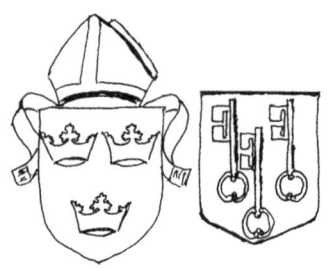

A Sea of Bishops,
A Forest of Deans

It is early, and I had not slept well. Poor excuse, really, but I found myself yawning as I waited in the Cathedral for the early Eucharist to start. I looked round: the usual suspects, all of us well gone in years: old John, who has the next allotment to mine, who grew up within a hundred yards or so of where his strawberries grow to red and scented splendour; the devout lady who always wears black, and a hood that looks like a wimple, who clearly knows the liturgy by heart; the man with two sticks who cannot kneel. (I wonder what figure I would make in someone else's prose, for I too am old and have my eccentricities...) 'It's only the old who go to church...' you hear that so often. Up to a point, it's mainly true.

But the old have been through all that the changes and chances this fleeting life can throw at them, and yet come here to fold their wings for a space, to find that peace the world gives no one. Life and much experience have led them here, to the still centre of the turning world. But the younger folk cannot stay: they must be on their way to work through the usual, tediously awful, traffic. What a way for them, poor things, to start the day... My mind is wandering ('Don't worry', Father Robert says, 'just bring it back gently to where you want it to be.' All very well...) The array of hassocks is colourful, for they are decorated with embroidered arms, dates and initials of various notables and bishops. I idly scan them, trying to read the achievements of arms (some of these bishops lived before there was any systematic heraldry to speak of, but that makes no matter) and identify them. Some of them do have a part in the story – this story – and a context into which I can put them. But there are so many. I feel often I am drowning in a sea of bishops, lost in a forest of deans...

Knowledge of, familiarity with, affection for this Cathedral has accrued over the years, rather like a fugue, where the initial idea is developed and seen in new ways, put in new contexts by every succeeding entry, without the original idea ever quite disappearing. How do you remember when you first found *that* out, or that? How were you different? And to get to what you are seeing now, all the different moods and states of mind you were in when you came on those irregular visits over many years have contributed. One evening – one of the worst of my life – of utter desolation, days of delight, make a polyphony or rather a symphony, that resounds as once more you push open the door and feel past you the mighty rush of air that you have let into the vast space. I remember my mother seeing the long nave for the first time, and falling awed into rare silence; and my father, well overweight and not good on his legs, being pushed by my son in the Cathedral wheelchair – a wicker affair, which had seen many days, and which always stood by the West Door for the use of those who needed it. My son pushed him down that same nave at as much speed as his young legs could go. I don't think my father had a chance to look up at L'Estrange's and Gambier Parry's painted ceiling of the ancestry of Jesus from Adam to Mary. (The lad made a tight turn under the Octagon – no nave altar then, and the mediaeval pulpitum closing off the monk's part of the church from where the laity could go was removed in the eighteenth century – and came haring back. My rebuke was ready primed, but my father's smile defused it.) It is indeed a tempting space, and there were no chairs set out then. Unsurprisingly, between 1725 and 1763, the boys of The King's School were allowed to play games in the nave, to spin tops, to roll hoops, when the weather was too poor to play outside.

Much later, scored into the memory, when Rosanna and I were first able to overnight in the partly refurbished house, there was an evening of extreme frost, when we came, muffled up in overcoats, to the Lady Chapel to hear a remarkable group of young men, just out of university, singing Byrd and Tallis, with their rising breath misting the air: the Gesualdo Six, at the beginning of their great career, and hearing for the first time the lovely bass of their leader Owain Park: a voice as rich as Guinness. If voices had colours, Owain's would be the colour of that noble drink. Another memory: my granddaughter and I at Evensong, to which she had never before been, and she palpably overwhelmed by the singing and the organ: 'Was there just *one* man playing?', she asked. There was another Evensong when at the end the organ thundered forth a voluntary from Boëllmann's *Suite Gothique* which had everyone jolly and smiling as they went out in the winter dark; and a funeral when the tragic – for once the word is right – loss of a fine young cleric, a great pastor and teacher, gathered together 200 clergy and about 700 laity, and not one of us was not in tears. To grieve together is to begin the healing, but it does not lessen the loss.

Visitors to the House in Cow Lane are often offered 'Tea and Evensong', or 'Evensong and Drinks'. After all, even if the noble and gracious words of the Office leave one cold and wondering what all the fuss is about, a first-class choir singing serious music on your doorstep is hardly something at which to turn up your nose.

I was once a choirboy in a large village church, led by a very ambitious choirmaster. Three sung services on a Sunday were just normal to me as I grew from a little and probably tiresome lad in short trousers to a youth with the beginning of a moustache – which is when they said to me, 'You can be an altar boy if you must but *please* don't sing.' (I was mortified for decades. And kept silent.) I had no idea we were singing Bach, and Handel, and Mendelssohn, and Stainer and Stanford and Wesley and… I just got on with it and loved it. I had no idea what many of the psalms were on about – *then* – but later, how

I valued that exposure to them and grew to appreciate the riches of the Hebrew poetry in the majestic prose of Miles Coverdale's 1549 translation! All unawares, I was getting the groundings of an education in music, and literature, and you cannot help but learn a lot of history in a place whose beauty, changing with the light of the seasons, affects you in ways you may not understand. You also learn to work with other people, in a mutually supportive group. So to go through real choir school, day by day, as do some of the boys and girls at Ely's King's School is to get a wonderful education almost without noticing it. You grow into it, people tell me, as your capacity for thought and understanding grow, and having been a choral scholar marks you for life.

We often sit in the choir stalls on the north, where we can see the light of the westering sun shine through the windows of the south-west face of the Octagon – an unusual angle for the sun in any church – and once again tell the unchanging story of the stained glass. If you go over a period of time you see the boys and girls visibly growing, becoming more confident, graduating to doing a solo part and sending their lone voice down the immensity of the nave, and then falling back into the community of voices. For some, when they start, before they are admitted to the dignity of Chorister by the Dean and can put a white surplice over their red cassock, it is all clearly a bit daunting. Even well on in the autumn term, some of the very young ones still have to find their feet, or voices: one little boy, sandwiched between two tall and confident lads, clearly just got fed up and kept his mouth shut for everything except the preces. Another time, a lad, clearly new, sitting with (I think) his mother slightly away from the choir, wore a red cassock slightly too big for him ('He'll grow into it' – how I impotently fumed when I heard that said by a shop assistant to one of my parents!) and spent the whole service gazing up in what looked like wonder at the vault of the presbytery. He did not try to sing. That will come.

They say Edward the Confessor was a boy at the Cathedral school, that preceded Henry VIII's refoundation of it as The King's School. It is not impossible, indeed.

The building has become almost a daily sight. The initial awe at sight of the building towering up at the end of Palace Green has softened into a sort of familiarity, affection. It has become a place of friends – yes, real living ones, whose voices you know, whose illnesses you care about – but also a long perspective of the dead, whom you can never hear but with whose stories you have become familiar enough, over many years, for them to be part of your own memory, to be moving, or to make you cross, or grieve, or be appalled. Those people once lived and breathed as do we, and were as contradictory and confused and faced with impossible choices as are we.

The silent monuments speak: even a single word, 'Byrthnoth', hardly noticeable it is so small and hidden, can send my mind hurtling back to a bloody morning by a tidal creek. An empty cenotaph can make me grieve for some of the best blood in England shed by a man, proudly portrayed between two of his three wives, who was also a humanist and a scholar and one of the best educated laymen of his generation. (Like widely read

Stalin having a personal library of some 20,000 books, or Hitler correcting Furtwängler on the scoring of Wagner's *Das Rheingold*).

A lot of visitors do come to the House in Cow Lane, ranging from students of mine having a break from Cambridge to travellers from far lands and long ago. (Years ago my dear friend Henry St J. Hart, by then well on in years, gave me wise advice, with a touch of cynicism: 'When you are growing old, live where people will want to come, and not just to see you.' He took his own advice.) Nearly always, they want me to 'take them round the Cathedral'. I protest that I am no proper guide, and others could do it far better, but that I can introduce them to my personal delights and to some of those dead I call my friends. And I remind them that the beauty of this building, like any other great building of the Middle Ages, never made reductive economic sense: it was, in the last analysis, an act of worship, to the greater glory of God, even if some of the people having it built saw it as an act of personal glory and prestige and some of those working on it swore about the backbreaking and often dangerous work. And it cost lives: it is estimated – how verifiable that is I know not – that working on the building, at various dates in the Middle Ages, took the lives of 365 men. At Canterbury in 1177 when it was being built the architect (as we would call him) William of Sens slipped and fell from the scaffolding, and was badly injured. George Basevi (1794-1845), whose most important work is the Fitzwilliam Museum in Cambridge (1837), fell through the scaffolding to his death while inspecting the west tower of Ely in October 1845.

Timber scaffolding lashed together with rope. One poor knot… Health and Safety would have had a fit.

This wandering I do, as cicerone or not, round the great building, whose ground bass never goes away, with pauses to listen to what this thing or that has to say this time, is rather like hearing a version of Moussorgsky's *Pictures at an Exhibition*. Every bit of it has a story. If taking visitors new to the place round, I always start with Ovin, for the broken stones of the shaft of his cross in the south aisle are the oldest things in the building, and of Etheldreda's general manager there is much to say – if only we knew it all! I would give a lot to glimpse the personal relationship between them. In fact, this is not a bad place to fill in some of what floats about in my mind when I take the dog to St Ovin's Green for those last, important sniffs before bed.

The cross was not elaborate – I have seen far more flamboyant fragments of crosses of the same period treasured in parish churches across the north country that will never not be Home for me. Whether Ovin was a saint by the usual tests, who knows? Not for me to say. The stones came from Haddenham, where the Isle of Ely presents its steepest face to the encircling Fen, a prospect which daunted even William the Bastard when it was held against him. One was being used as a mounting block on a farm: why waste a good bit of stone even if it had been a cross? On it is an inscription, faint now: *LUCEM TUAM OVINO DA DEUS REQUIEM* AMEN – 'God, grant thy light and peace to Ovin. Amen.' And after 13 centuries he still has a place in the story, though he wrote no books, conquered no lands, and made small noise in the world save in the quiet humility of faithful service.

We can't piece together much of a biography from the not always consistent mentions in Bede's *Ecclesiastical History* and the much later *Liber Elienesis*. The usual account goes that he was probably born about 620 in the Fens. His people would have been the Gyrwas, and his name suggests he was of British rather than Anglian stock. It is said that his administrative ability was recognised so early that by the 640s he was managing a large chunk of the Fens for his prince Tondberct – that title is anachronistic, but let that pass. In 652 he first met Etheldreda, daughter of Anna, King of the East Angles, and niece of Raedwald, whose is almost certainly the great ship burial at Sutton Hoo. She was born, we think, in the royal demesne of Exning, a day's walk away, was deeply devout like her sisters, and despite a vow of perpetual virginity had been married at 16 to Tondberct for political and strategic reasons: her father needed that alliance to cover his western flank against an aggressive Mercia. Tondberct gave the Isle of 'Elge' – Ely – to his princess as a 'morning gift' – a sort of endowment on marriage, and a magnificent one, for the Isle is very rich. From this gift stems the status of the Isle of Ely as a Palatinate jurisdiction, whose Bishop was a prince whose peace it was you broke (if so inclined), rather than the King's.[24]

Tondberct died quite young – probably in 655, but certainly by 660 – and Etheldreda, having lost her father in battle with the formidable Penda, the pagan king of Mercia, made Ovin her steward and relied on him to manage her estate whilst she herself lived a religious life with a group of friends on the Isle.

But when soon afterwards Penda himself was killed at the battle of the Winwaed – we don't know exactly where that was, but it may have been near where the A1 traffic thunders over the bridge of the Went valley – the two great Christian Kingdoms of Northumbria and East Anglia could draw closer together. Royal women were as good as a treaty: in 660 Etheldreda was 'persuaded' to cement this alliance more firmly and travelled north to marry the teenage Ecgfrith, heir to Northumbria. Ovin, as the 'chief of her servants', as Bede calls him, would have managed her journey to the wedding, conducted by (St) Wilfrid in York. This ill-matched union inevitably failed, and with the mediation of Archbishop Wilfrid it was agreed that Ecgfrith should find another wife and Etheldreda should become a nun in a monastery run by (St) Æbbe at Coldingham, north of Berwick.*

Ovin presented himself to Abbott (St) Chad at his monastery at Lastingham, carrying a spade and mattock: he came to do humble manual work in that monastery. The two men got on: when Chad was made Abbot of Lichfield, Ovin went south with him as one of his monks. But Chad died in 672, just when Etheldreda was coming back to Ely to establish a double monastery for monks and nuns. Ovin supposedly (and it is wholly plausible) came over to help with the practical business of building her Abbey. Six years later, in 679, Etheldreda died. Ovin would be in his late fifties, and it would be nice to think he retired to the monastery he had helped build. But he never saw this one: his was wooden, and not even on this site.

---

* Æbbe was the sister of (St) Oswald and Oswiu, who convened the Synod of Whitby.

I do love being able to think of a real person of flesh and blood when I look at his stone: and I do pray for his peace.

I used, in days when the Cathedral seemed to be less busy with visitors, to make a beeline for the choir stalls, moved to their present position from under the octagon when James Essex (a sensible if not first rank architect) demolished the mediaeval pulpitum which divided the monk's part of the church from where the laity could go. (It would have been reverently protected three generations later. It was at the western end of the space under the Octagon. I am rather glad Essex moved it.) I used to take the more bendable of my visitors there, to see the misericords, those merciful ledges under the tip-up seats on which a tired monk could rest his bottom during the long chanting of the psalms of the day. To appreciate the wit and grotesquerie, and symbolism, of the carvings entails crawling under the desks, preferably with a torch. I stopped after one visit when we were doing just that, and a voice above my head sternly said, 'Just what do you think you are doing?' I wriggled upright and said, 'I just wanted to show them the mermaid.' I got a very odd look indeed, and an injunction that permission must be sought before any such frivolous activity be repeated. So I give mermaids and the fox preaching to a cock and two hens a miss now, just tell friends to go and look at them when they have time, and take them to something more dignified, like the tombstone cut in Tournai 'marble' (actually, black limestone) of Bishop Nigel, Treasurer of England, and Bishop from 1133 to 1169, over the whole troublous Anarchy of the War between King Stephen and the Empress Matilda.[25]

That awful time was when the chronicler in Peterborough, writing as it was all happening, recorded that such was the suffering that 'people said Christ and his saints slept.' A Bishop then was a major lay magnate as well as a spiritual overseer, and the strain, and danger, of negotiating this period of changing alliances and allegiances is beyond imagining. Nigel's tombstone has at its head a carving of a clearly substantial Romanesque building, which alludes to the work he did on the building of the Cathedral where what is mortal of him lies. Below, held gently in a scarf, a naked, ungendered soul is being carried up to Heaven by the Archangel Michael, who had by that time been given the job the Ancients gave to the god Mercury as psychopomp, or guider of souls. It would have been impossible to keep one's hands clean in his job, and I do hope Nigel found peace. (He had little from the monks of his chapter, for they thought he was keeping money for himself that by rights belonged to them.)

He, and his uncle Roger, Bishop of Salisbury had a hard time when Stephen acceded to the uncertain throne when Henry I died. Henry had made Nigel Treasurer, but Stephen kicked him out and Nigel defected to his enemy Matilda. It is a sorry tale, of treachery, being besieged in his castle of Devizes, and then, after a fragile peace was broken, in the Isle of Ely which he fortified against the King, then imprisoned (with his uncle) and put in chains by a vengeful Stephen… He survived to see Matilda's son Henry established as king, and was once more given high office.

Most people are surprised, and some a little shocked, when I tell them that, like his uncle Bishop Roger, Nigel had a wife, and sons, who themselves made a noise in the world. (One of them, Richard, wrote the first treatise on the Exchequer, the *Dialogus de Scaccario*.)

Moussorgsky in my mind's ears at least, we move a few yards and I tip my hat to Bishop John Alcock. He was a persuasive man, who managed to get Pope Alexander VI (father of Cesare and Lucrezia Borgia) and Henry VII to agree to him suppressing the failing Benedictine nunnery of St Radegund by Midsummer Common in Cambridge, and founding in its stead a college of graduate priests studying for degrees in theology: Jesus College. (As it happens, the final legal steps of its foundation were only completed by Bishop Nicholas West, sixteen years after Alcock died in 1500.) One of its first students and Fellows was Thomas Cranmer, the first Protestant Archbishop of Canterbury. John Bale, who overlapped with Cranmer at Jesus College, wrote, when Alcock had been dead some twenty years, that he 'devoted himself from childhood to learning and piety [and] made such a proficiency in virtue that no one in England had a greater reputation for sanctity.' Bale, erstwhile Carmelite friar, bitter controversialist indispensable to Thomas Cromwell, provocative playwright and finally Bishop of Ossory, did not give praise lightly: he was nicknamed 'bilious Bale' because of his bad temper and habit of getting into rows.

Alcock, like Nicholas West, was never far from the higher echelons of government or from its Europe-wide network: the very rich Bishopric of Ely was in both cases the reward of a grateful Crown. Alcock was mostly based in England, working in legal administration and royal building programmes ('the King's Works'); West was often abroad on diplomatic missions.[26]

Alcock and West were hardworking, and effective, managers as bishops, which did not stop them being devout. Each had provided for the establishing of a chantry chapel in the Cathedral where a priest could be retained to say masses for the repose of their souls, and their passage through Purgatory. In 1500, when Alcock died, the storm of Reformation was in the future, and unimaginable; West died in 1533, and a handful of years later his superlatively lovely chapel and all it stood for was on the wrong side of politics and ideology.

The Cathedral was surrendered by the Prior and Chapter to Henry VIII's Commissioners on 18th November 1539. A House that at its height had had more than a hundred monks and lay brothers now had only 23. The church was 'cleansed': most of the statuary, carvings, brasses and stained-glass windows were destroyed, for they were 'graven images'. The last Prior, Robert Steward, who seems to have been sympathetic to, or at least prepared to accept the proceedings, secured his own future as first Dean of the Cathedral. Henry re-endowed the school as The King's School. The huge Lady Chapel, one of the glories of English architecture built to honour the now politically incorrect Virgin Mother of Christ, languished without glass or the candlelight playing on the life and miracles of the Virgin told in the polychrome narrative of the wondrously delicate carving, as you followed it round the building. It became the parish church of Holy Trinity, and remained so right through to the twentieth century.

All that was in the future. Alcock made sure people could not forget for whom the chapel was made: his rebus, a cock, is in many places, in glass and stone. (It is also on the arms of Jesus College.) The statues that once graced its niches have all gone, of course, probably dourly burnt for lime as idolatrous. The lavish ebullience of its structure remains: if stone could effloresce, it would look like this. But it sits ill with the more restrained style of the space in which it has been plonked: that is the right word, for indeed some think that it was designed and prefabricated for another space altogether, possibly Worcester, where he was bishop for ten years before being translated to Ely. (I do like the idea of pre-fabricated chantries.) It was one of my pupils years ago who pointed out what I had never noticed, that the front has had to be trimmed and squeezed to fit the width of the aisle. As soon as it's pointed out, it's obvious. But I missed it for years.

Sometimes, the early Eucharist has been in Bishop West's chapel, lovely, though now only a shade of the subtle glory the Reformers wrecked. Everywhere I look, as we wait for the Eucharist to begin, I see Nicholas West's motto, which he chose from St Paul (I Cor. 15.10): *Dei gratia sum id quod sum* – 'by the grace of God I am what I am.' I wonder why he chose this. 'Hasn't God been good to me in giving me this plum bishopric!'? 'Haven't I done well, when once I was merely a little boy on the Foundation at Eton!'? And he did build himself a most magnificent and unignorable chantry in a soufflé of late Gothic structure and up to the minute urbane Italian Renaissance detail. Traces of the paint survive, that once would have seemed to move and change colour as the flames of the permanently burning candles moved in a flaw of air. 'By the Grace of God I am what I am': I like to think he was deliberately ambiguous. Perhaps it was real humility, just as the monks say Thomas Becket, proud prelate, was wearing a hair shirt under the magnificence of archiepiscopal majesty. Perhaps he is implying, 'I accept my faults, for even they can work to the glory of God. Even in my brokenness, God has a use for me, even that brokenness may be part of the purpose; yes, his mercy is over all.' Yes, but the mercy of God is no excuse for us not trying.

One morning, knowing I was going to do one of my long walks, the Bishop's Chaplain gave me that gracious Irish blessing after the Eucharist:

> *'May the road rise up to meet you.*
> *May the wind be always at your back.*
> *May the sun shine warm upon your face;*
> *the rains fall soft upon your fields*
> *and until we meet again, may God hold you in the palm*
> *of His hand.'*

We were both moved. We said little. Rosanna set off for her work in the clinic, and I set off to walk to Cambridge. It does not matter why.

On the south wall of the chapel there is a tomb chest, with a sort of *omnium gatherum* of bits of bygone bishops, mainly Saxon. Neatly tidied away – after all, our ancestors were quite happy with charnel houses, where you indiscriminately dumped the bones of corpses after they had been buried for some time in the churchyard. (I once went into one – disused and empty now, of course – in a church in the Forest of Dean, and picked up a tooth. It was someone's premolar: s/he was old because it had worn flat with eating stone-ground bread. Times do elide for me rather often…) But among the bishops, I saw, that first time I went into that chapel, with a sort of start, a name I recognised: a man about whose heroic death at Maldon in 991 men told tales and made poems, one of which I had read in the ancient tongue of this island. Sometimes, the reminders of the bloodiness that is always just in the shadows, hit you...

Byrthnoth... The fine Old English poem, *The Battle of Maldon*, tells the tale of the fight at the ford where fell brave Byrthnoth, ealdorman of Essex done to death by dire Danes. Headless they hewed him, mourned by his men... His men brought his body – the head they found never – back to the Abbey at Ely, whence he and his band had gone forth to battle. The Abbot and his people buried him with due honour, a ball of wax doing duty for his head.

They were bloody times indeed. There were more to come. Somewhere in the Cathedral lies the body of Ælfræd Ætheling – Prince Alfred. It's not a pretty story, but not untypical of what humans bent on power can do to each other. (Now...) He was the youngest son of Æthelræd II Unræde by Emma of Normandy: his elder brother was Edward, known later as the Confessor, who, so some say – including the 12th century *Liber Eliensis* – had been a boy in the choir school that is the ultimate ancestor of The King's School. Æthelræd became king in 978 when he was just 12 – 'Woe to the land whose king is a child!', as The Preacher warns in Ecclesiastes 10.16 – after his elder half-brother, St Edward, King and Martyr, was murdered, probably with the connivance of Æthelræd's mother Ælfþrith. For the next 37 years, until he died in 1016, he had a tough hand to play, and historical memory has not treated him well. He had some ability and lots of bad luck: his nickname ought to not be Unready, which suggests mere lackadaisical disorganisation, so much as 'Ill-advised' (true enough), or 'without counsel'. Throughout all Æthelræd's reign, his chief headache was the incursions of the Danes. For after nine decades of (more or less) peace, the Danes had resumed serious raiding in the 980s. After the fall of Byrthnoth at Maldon in 991 Æthelræd was forced to pay them yearly tribute: Danegeld. In 1013, the Danish king, Sweyn Forkbeard, again invaded England, and Æthelræd fled to Normandy. When Sweyn died in 1014, Æthelræd ventured back, but died two years later. His eldest son, Edmund Ironside, was briefly king, but died after a few months and was succeeded by Sweyn's son Knut – Canute. Knut of Denmark was one of the most dangerous, determined and efficient operators around. He collected kingdoms – Sweden, Norway, England – like others collect blackberries. The *Anglo Saxon Chronicle* gives the background to Aelfred's story after Knut/Canute died in 1028 at Shaftesbury.

> *... on the second day before the ides of November; and he is buried at Winchester in the Old Minster. He was king over all England very near twenty winters. Soon after his death, there was a council of all the nobles at Oxford; wherein Earl Leofric, and almost all the thanes north of the Thames, and the men of the ships in London, chose Harald [Knut's son, called Harefoot] to govern all England, for himself and his brother Harðacanute, who was in Denmark. Earl Godwin, and all the eldest men in Wessex, withstood it as long as they could; but they could do nothing...*

Æthelræd's younger sons, Alfred and his elder brother Edward 'the Confessor', had been deprived their birthrights by their mother's second marriage to Knut, and they were brought up in Normandy. Emma was living on her estates in Winchester. Norman sources say Edward had first tried to join their mother in Winchester in 1036, sailing up the Solent and winning a battle near Southampton before returning to Normandy with his plunder (he was not quite the wishy-washy person of popular history.) Later that year Alfred, probably in his late twenties, arrived in England. He may have been intending to meet his mother in Winchester, but it was assumed he would make a play for the crown. However, before he had chance to see Emma, Godwin, now supporting Harald Harefoot, met him with apparent welcome, and took him to his estate at Guildford. There his retinue were slaughtered: their mutilated remains were found by chance in 1929. Alfred was tied onto a horse and sent off to Ely, surrounded by water and its fens, treacherous and impassable to those who did not know the paths. On landing, his guards put out his eyes and tortured him. Though tended by the monks, he died soon afterwards.

The Chronicle here breaks into verse:

> *Ac Godwine hine þa gelette   and hine on hæft sette,*
> *and his geferan he todraf,   and sume mislice ofsloh;*
> *sume hi man wið feo sealde,   sume hreowlice acwealde,*
> *sume hi man bende,   sume hi man blende,*
> *sume hamelode,   sume hættode.*
> *Ne wearð dreorlicre dæd   gedon on þison earde,*
> *syþþan Dene comon   and her frið namon*
> *Nu is to gelyfenne   to ðan leofan gode,*
> *þæt hi blission   bliðe mid Criste*

þe wæron butan scylde   swa earmlice acwealde.
Se æpeling lyfode þa gyt;   ælc yfel man him gehet,
oðþæt man gerædde   þæt man hine lædde
to Eligbyrig   swa gebundenne.
Sona swa he lende,   on scype man hine blende,
and hine swa blindne   brohte to ðam munecon,
and he þar wunode   ða hwile þe he lyfode.
Syððan hine man byrigde,   swa him wel gebyrede,
ful wurðlice,   swa he wyrðe wæs,
æt þam westende,   þam styple ful gehende,
on þam suðportice;   seo saul is mid Criste.

But Godwin then caught him and him captive made,
and cast his companions aside. Some variously he slew;
some as slaves sold, some cruelly killed,
some bound, and some of sight blinded,
some he hamstrung and scalped he some.
No more dreadful deed was in this land done
since the Danes came and with us dealt peace.
Now we should trust in the dear God
That joyfully with Christ they rejoice,
Clean of evil they were, so cruelly killed.
Yet lived the prince – men promised him bale –
until carls counselled that he be carried
to Ely borough, bound as he was.
Yet when he came thither, on ship-board they
blinded him,
and brought him thus blind to the brothers,
with them he dwelt while his life dured.
They buried his body then as was but fitting,
full worthily, just as he was of worth full,
right near the steeple at the west end,
in the south portico: with Christ is his soul.[27]

I do not know where his grave is, but knowing his story, when it comes, as it does from time to time, into my mind, can shadow the sunlight though the windows. Sometimes I shiver. And think of Yemen, and the Uighurs, and Ukraine, and Gaza, and…

I always leave Bishop West's chapel with some reluctance: that lovely space always helps the mind to quieten. But as you do leave, on your right is what looks like a massive tomb chest. It is actually an empty cenotaph, and on it, high so you can't actually look at them, lie the effigies of Sir John Tiptoft, first Earl of Worcester, and two of his three wives. (He is actually buried in Blackfriars in London.) They look, so far as one *can* see them, calm, pious, peaceful. He had connections here: a relative, Sir John Tiptoft of Burwell, the next village to Reach, was Speaker in Parliament in 1406 and had a long career in government. He is buried somewhere hereabouts.

But the earl, descendant of Charlemagne, Henry III, and Llewellyn the Great, distinguished himself in other ways. He studied at University College, Oxford, collected high offices from the Crown with panache, went on pilgrimage to the Holy Land, and on the way back spent two years acquiring a reputation as a fine scholar at the University of Padua. He got back in 1461 and was in high favour with Edward IV who had deposed the Lancastrian Henry VI: Edward gave him the Garter, then the offices of Constable of the Tower for life, Lord Steward of the Household, Lord High Constable. And his actions in that last office are what is remembered. He personally presided over 'trials' of the Yorkist Edward's Lancastrian enemies, which always resulted in attainder and execution, which he carried out with exceptional, gratuitous cruelty. Some men were beheaded, some hung till nearly dead, then cut down, disembowelled while still just alive, and then hacked into quarters to symbolise how a traitor dismembered the Body Politic. Some were impaled. Edward promoted him to be Chancellor and later Lord Deputy (viceroy) of Ireland, where he had Thomas FitzGerald, Earl of Desmond executed. But in 1470 Lancastrian Henry VI was briefly restored to the throne. Edward and his court fled abroad, but Tiptoft could not make his escape in time. The Lancastrians took their revenge on the man who had become known as the Butcher of England. That was not a name that could be given without his having been exceptional in those terrible decades of the kinstrife when the English aristocracy almost destroyed itself, leaving the way ahead open for the lawyers and the parvenus who did well out of the upstart Tudors.

Tiptoft was beheaded in the Tower. He asked the headsman to do it with three stokes of the axe, in honour of the Holy Trinity... As one might say, get your head round that.

Almost opposite is Bishop Peter Gunning's memorial. His epitaph is fulsome in its praise of his virtues and his achievements, finally as Bishop from 1675-84. It would say that, wouldn't it? Funeral monuments are not critical assessments. But he lived through interesting times: a bloody Civil War (which cost, according to one estimate, upwards of 200,000 lives: 4% of the estimated population of England in 1651), Protectorate, military dictatorship, war with the Dutch, the Restoration of Charles II and the revanchism (much against that wise monarch's wishes) of the Cavalier Parliament, and he died just in time to avoid the tumultuous days of James II's short reign and deposition. Gunning was Royalist, and so Parliament ejected him from his Fellowship of Clare College, Cambridge in 1644. He went to be chaplain of New College, Oxford, but was turfed out of there when Oxford fell to the Parliamentarians. During the Protectorate of Cromwell he made a living as tutor and chaplain to a number of Royalist families: not an easy alternative for an Anglican divine, for as John Evelyn's diary reminds you, the Offices of the Church of England had to be held in secret, behind closed, locked doors. There was always the fear of betrayal to the thought police. At the Restoration he returned to Cambridge as Lady Margaret Professor of Divinity, became Master of Corpus Christi College, and later Master of St. John's. In 1670 Charles made him Bishop of Chichester, and in 1675 Bishop of Ely.

That sort of career is not without parallel in those troubled times. But it is his effigy that always grabs my attention. I have rarely seen an effigy look so uncomfortable. He is reclining, propped up as if in bed, on his left arm. His legs are crossed. His neat Van Dyck beard and moustache are immaculate. And he is wearing his mitre. Seeing it for the first time my daughter said, 'Why is that man wearing that funny nightcap?' A good question... As sometimes early modern men and women commissioned their funeral monuments well before they died, I can't help wondering about sitting for a portrait. Uncomfortable.

By this time, many of my victims are getting bored or impatient (indeed, you may be too) and somewhat reluctantly – for there is more (oh, much, much more!) I stop and lead them out through the south door into the ghost of the cloister, with some tiny shreds of the mediaeval glass – a bit of angel, a hint of the face of a female saint – gracing the windows. I can't resist pointing out how one of the new – well, they were in the 1320s – piers for the octagon has swallowed up part of a Norman doorway which the monks would have used on their way from the dorter to sing the Offices of Matin and Lauds, woken by the bell in the darkness of the small hours. But often my companions' eyes are caught not by that but by the memorial poem, 'The Spiritual Railway', to those two men who were killed in that railway accident in 1845 on the Norwich–Ely line. Often indulgent smiles appear at the quality of the verse and naivety of the symbolism: but I often wonder whether it makes any of them think – perhaps much, much later?

In the carved boss on the vault of the roof a swallow regularly makes her summer nest – or used to. 'Yea the swallow hath found her a nest where she may lay her young, even thine altars, O Lord.' Psalm 84 is a favourite, happy and wholly appropriate as we come out into the sunlight. Ahead is the huge old tithe barn which the monastery built in its heyday to store its dues paid in kind, and beyond that is the Motte which William the Bastard's men may well have raised up when they besieged the Abbey during Hereward the Wake's stubborn resistance. The monks capitulated when they saw the siege engines being assembled. (William was devout enough in the monastery, but fined the community an eyewatering sum for their erstwhile defiance.) So there was never a stone castle there, only for centuries a peaceable, useful windmill. Gone now, and the old bailey of the castle[28] where once preparation for war and sack was made is a place for children and happy dogs like Milo and youths up to mild mischief. The once elegant monument on the top, which you can reach with determination (if so inclined), through the thickets, by a spiralling path shown on Speed's 1610 map, has had the attention of the wanton destructiveness which seems to be somehow embedded in what it is to be young and male and in company.

The Lincoln red polls graze in season in the Dean's Meadow. They occasionally will pass the time of day with you by the gate. Cowpats crust over in the heat of the sun. The beasts shelter, head to swishing tail, from the heat under the kindly tent of the oriental plane. Bishop Gunning planted its noble cousin across the road, in the garden of the old Bishop's Palace. Its hairy, insignficant spring flowers become, as the year ages, dangles of ball-like pods containing hundreds of little winged seeds. Gunning's tree has grown to be, people say, the largest in England. I do not know whether it has pupped. I hope so.

But as I come out of what was the cloister into the open air below the sundial,[*] I will often not look ahead at the noble prospect but glance up to where the peregrines sometimes nest, for a Cathedral is a marvellous artificial

---

[*] It offers good advice: KAIPON ΓΝΩΘΙ –'Know the right time', or, better, 'Know when the time is right'.

cliff, and peregrines rely on a fast stoop from above.[29] I love those noble birds. There was one early morning, Ascensiontide, when I had gone on my own and came out to the pouring rain that we had heard on the roof all during the service. (Rosanna wisely had decided that she needed to do things at the house.) Outside stood a bedraggled, heterogeneous, knot of people, one with a really serious camera with a long lens, gazing up into heaven… I could scarce restrain myself from saying, in the words of the Ascensiontide antiphon, 'Ye men of Galilee, why stand ye gazing up into Heaven?'. Mummy had just killed – a woodpigeon, by the look of it. (And pigeon breast lightly roasted stuffed with black pudding is wonderful… not that I am suggesting that is peregrine fare.) She was on the parapet high up, tearing the bird to bits for her three chicks, who had the untidy 'unmade bed' look half fledged young birds do have. Far from waiting patiently for their turn, they were visibly squabbling, pushing each other out of the way. Meanwhile, at the other end of the parapet, his back resolutely turned to this domestic mayhem, Daddy sat with shoulders hunched. But then, they had both been up early, for they hunt mostly soon after dawn and before dusk.

Once, in Norway, I had seen a pair in their spectacular aerobatic courtship, fast, precise spirals, and steep dives during which the smaller tiercel will pass gifts of prey to the formel in mid-flight. She will actually fly upside-down to take the food from her lover's talons. To think that this happens in Ely most years, and most people pass on unaware.

I only recently found out that peregrines only hit about 10-20% of the birds they stoop at – they reach speeds of

320kmh – but if they miss, will chase prey in a twisting flight. Here's where a pigeon's extraordinary aerial agility pays off: they can sometimes get away, while the kinetic energy of the peregrine's speed makes turning hard.

Sometimes. Below, on the grass in the angle of the transept and the choir, by the few gravestones, lay a wing bone with a pigeon feather attached to it.

Rain was dripping down my neck. But what a bonus to start the day!

By chance, on the secondhand bookstall in the market I came across a late edition of the *Journeys of Celia Fiennes*. She is not quite a household name, but this interesting lady, granddaughter of William Fiennes, Lord Saye and Sele, one of the important Parliamentary leaders in the Civil War, travelled for pleasure when nobody much did, 'to regain my health by variety and change of aire and exercise'. She thought that

> *...if all persons, both Ladies, much more Gentlemen, would spend some of their time in Journeys to visit their native Land, and be curious to inform themselves and make observations of the pleasant prospects, good buildings, different produces and manufactures of each place ... would be a souveraign remedy to cure or preserve ffrom these Epidemick diseases of vapours, should I add Laziness?*

(I am doing my best, dear lady.) She covered a lot of England, and left a delightful and quirky account of her tours. She came to Ely in 1698, on her journey from Cambridge to Lichfield, and her account is probably the very first account of the town and Cathedral by what we would call a tourist:

There are two Churches. Ely Minster is a curious pile of building all of stone, the outside full of Carvings and great arches, and fine pillars in the front, and the inside has the greatest variety and neatness in the works. There are two Chappels, most exactly carv'd in stone, all sorts of figures, Cherubims Gilt, and painted in some parts. Ye Roofe of one Chappell was One Entire stone most delicately Carv'd and hung down in great poynts all about ye Church. The pillars are Carv'd and painted with ye history of the bible, especially the new testament and description of Christ's miracles. The Lanthorn in ye quire are vastly high and delicately painted, and fine Carv'd work all of wood. In it ye bells used to be hung [five]; *the demention* [dimension] *of ye biggest was so much that when they rung thm it shooke ye quire so, and ye Carv'd worke, that it was thought unsafe; therefore they were taken down. There is one Chappel for Confession, with a Roome and Chaire of State for ye priest to set to hear ye people on their knees Confess into his Eare through a hole in ye wall. This Church has ye most popish remaines of any I have seen.* [She was of a stoutly Protestant family.] *There still remains a Cross over the alter; the Candlesticks are 3 quarters of a yard high, massy silver gilt, very heavy. The ffont is One Entire piece of White Marble, stemm and foote; the Cover was Carv'd Wood, with ye image of Christ's being baptised by John, and the holy Dove descending on him, all finely Carv'd white wood, without any paint or varnish.*

But the town did not impress her. First, the journey from Newmarket led her to the causeway from Stuntney, but like everywhere else it was flooded and she had to use a boat. Then 'you ascend a very steep hill', and at the top she found 'the dirtiest place I ever saw, not a bit of pitching [stone paving] in the streets. So it's a perfect quagmire'. She saw many rats in the streets, and though her room at her inn – probably the Lamb (which had after all been going since 1416) as that was the best inn in the town – was up 20 steps, it was infested with 'frogs, slow-worms and snails'. The people she thought 'slothful' and the town a mess, for its Bishop, then Dr Simon Patrick, (who built the country house I covet most of all, Dalham Hall near Newmarket),

does not care to stay long in this place, not being good for his health; he is Lord of all the island, has the command and ye jurisdiction.... There is a good palace for the Bishop built, but it was unfurnished'

Well, it would be: at that period most people of high status took their furniture and effects with them when they to their other houses.

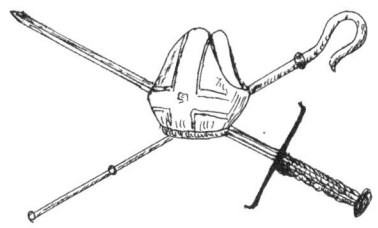

Power and the People

Few things are more peaceful, apparently, than animals contentedly grazing in a sunny paddock. 'They' make postcards of such scenes.

Where do elderly racehorses go when their race is run? (On second thoughts, in too many cases you might not like the answer to that question.) But I know two lucky ones who have been given a retirement home by two ladies who are passionate about their animals but are not that bothered about riding them. And by good fortune the two animals, who had not met before they shared a field, do get on together. Not all horses do, for they have their likes and dislikes just as we do. I recall one pair, years ago, when my daughter had her pony, who always stood at opposite ends of their field and ignored each other.

Now, these two are very handsome, long legged, graceful and affable animals. But I don't think they are of the brightest. Would you be, if all you had to stretch your mind was to run, day after day, a very boring course as fast as you can, and then stop? I was taking the dog past their field this afternoon, and saw that they had been given a toy: a large rubber ball, the size of a football. As Milo was busy being Milo, I stopped and leaned on my stick to watch. Clearly I was coming in in mid-game. One was nudging the ball with the off fore hoof, when the other came in in a neat manoeuvre from the side and grabbed the ball with its teeth. I don't know whether picking up the ball was against any rules, but the first horse was clearly shocked, as legend has it was the opposing side when William Webb Ellis as a boy at Rugby in 1823 picked up the ball and ran with it during a school football match. (And so, they say, rugby was born.) The horse now holding the ball just stood there, for all the world as if saying, 'Well, so what are you going to do about it?' First horse, stock still, thinks for a moment, then tries to grab the ball too: and does. The ball is getting less rotund by this time. Deadlock. Neither seems to know what to do. But then second horse (I ought to know their names, but don't) spots me by the fence, resigns the ball, and begins to come slowly over to me and Milo, whom they both quite like. (Milo, on the other hand, is not quite sure…). First horse is now in possession, drops the ball, and stands looking down at it where it unbouncily lies at his feet. Then just goes off for a mouthful of nice refreshing grass.

It makes you wonder whether the desire for possession for the sake of possession, which in humans has had so baleful an effect on the world, is not limited only to humans. But given our opposable thumbs and intelligence, we do far more damage. In human societies, alas, mayhem and bloodshed in always just below the surface, waiting in the shadows for the veneer of civility to wear thin and fray. Too many of our species welcome that, as the shameful shouts of the tabloids and the antics of too many people in power (or aspiring to it) indicate – and encourage. Somewhere near where in season foodstalls and happy fairs make the Green before the Cathedral full of life and laughter and the delicious smell of fried onions and hamburgers, the Danes in 870 slaughtered the monks and pillaged the monastery. The impassive stone of the west front has been wreathed in other smoke, other smells: the smoke of the fires of faith, and the smell of roast flesh: human. Everywhere is bloodstained: and thank God most of us have been lucky enough to have lived in an interim when the air, here at least, has been relatively sweet. Don't take it for granted.

It's not an obtrusive object, and it is quite easy to miss the black and white oval memorial as you cross the road when making for the Green in front of the Cathedral after yet another visit to that civilised bookshop in the High Street. But the first time you do see it, it dims the sunlight and makes the wind a little colder: like when you focus in your mind what the Russian cannon, on which a child is happily sitting astride, was made for. And what a cannon ball does.

REFORMATION MARTYRS
NEAR THIS PLACE ON 16 OCTOBER 1555
WILLIAM WOLSEY
CONSTABLE OF WELNEY, UPWELL
AND OUTWELL
ROBERT PYGOT
PAINTER FROM WISBECH
WERE BURNT AT THE STAKE
FOR THEIR CHRISTIAN FAITH

This was the first year of Mary Tudor's reign, and she and her able minster Cardinal Pole were determined to return England to the Catholic fold and turn back the tide of often cruelly extreme Protestantism which her father's and brother's reigns had unleashed. One of the local Justices of the Peace had noticed that though Wolsey[30] was regularly seen at services in the parish church, he used to absent himself at the key points of Mass.

It was found that he had got hold of a copy of the banned English translation of the New Testament, probably smuggled from Holland, with which those little ports on the Well Stream had frequent contact, and had become convinced that the Roman doctrine of the Mass was contrary to Scripture. John Foxe, in his hagiographical *Actes and Monuments*, aka 'Book of Martyrs' (1563), says Wolsey was firmly told that as a layman he should not meddle in the scriptures. John Fuller, Chancellor of Ely, lent him a book by Thomas Watson, Bishop of Lincoln.[31] Wolsey read it, and marked where he disagreed. Fuller asked him to 'rule his tongue' and said he would see that he was let off severe

212

punishment. However, Wolsey defiantly declared that he must witness to the truth.

Pygot – who was probably what we could call a decorator – lived a few miles away. He was summoned before the Justices for not attending church, and he and Wolsey were sent to prison at Ely to be tried for heresy: which, if they did not recant, carried the sentence of death: burning at the stake. On 9th October they both appeared before Dr Fuller, and the Dean of Norwich, John Christopherson. When pressed about the doctrine of transubstantiation of the bread and wine in the Mass, Wolsey and Pygot replied 'The [Roman] sacrament of the altar is an idol and the natural body and blood of Christ are not present in the said sacrament.' They refused to recant, and so were condemned to death.

A week later they were burned on the Cathedral Green at Ely, the same day that Bishops Latimer and Ridley were burned in Oxford. The sentence of condemnation was read and a sermon preached, and then they were led out of the Cathedral and chained to the same stake. An officer carried several copies of the banned English New Testament, which were also to be put on the pyre. Wolsey called on God to forgive his enemies and the two men each grabbed a book and defiantly began reciting Psalm 106 ('O geue thankes vnto the LORDE, for he is gracious, and his mercy endureth for euer') as the fire took hold and the smoke choked them. Foxe says they 'received the fire most thankfully'. The smoke would have mingled with the peat smoke of the cooking fires of the town, and the smell of roasting would have carried on the wind for quite a distance. There would have been crowds to witness the spectacle.

It is horrible. But poor, not very clever, Mary was a mere amateur at execution compared to her dreadful father. Slightly less than 300 people – about 100 for each year of her short reign, which is bad enough in all conscience, at two a week – suffered. In her father's reign of 36 years, one plausible estimate is that 57,000 people were executed, often horribly by hanging, disembowelling (while still alive), and quartering, for opposing him. Many were his own kin. Under Mary's sister Elizabeth, some 183 Catholics (130 of them priests) were executed under her anti-Catholic legislation during the whole 45 years of her reign. Many more were imprisoned or exiled. The Pope, Pius V, a rather stupid man, had made things a lot worse by his 1570 Bull *Regnans in Excelsis* which called on all English Catholics to seek to depose the Queen. This made any Catholic – and Elizabeth was up to then quite good at letting sleeping dogs lie – into a potential traitor. Torture was also used in her reign more than in any other: and the name of the chief torturer, the sadistic Richard Topcliffe, is one of the deep blots on that clever woman's time.

And talking of confinement, imprisonment: Elizabeth was right to be afraid. Hers was the most insecure throne in Europe, and there were indeed several serious plots against her. She had to be careful. One of Northamptonshire's wealthier gentlemen, who made no secret of his Catholicism, was the prayerful and peaceable High Sheriff of the county, Thomas Tresham. He built the lovely Triangular Lodge at Rushton, which in its design and numerology and symbolism still today proclaims to all who can read his code – English Heritage helps – his firm devotion to the Blessed Virgin

Mary whose honouring was explicitly off limits. Openly recusant, fined many times,[*] the Queen's ministers – he knew Cecil and Hatton quite well – felt he had to be imprisoned. And so he was, honourably but firmly, four times in the palace at Ely. He would have walked in the Long Gallery to take his exercise and looked out over the spot where Protestant Wolsey and Pygot had been burned.

Just as we should never belittle the past by romanticising, mentally theme-parking it, so we should never think the present is any better. Think of the cannon and what it was for, and what is happening as I write this in Sinkiang or Ukraine or Yemen or Gaza. Human nature remains the same, and all ideologies where people are certain of the exclusivity of their truth can be toxic. We have no room to talk.

'Littleport? That's where the riots were,' someone once said to me when I had asked whether Littleport was interesting enough to deserve a visit. (It is.) I was still new to this area, then, and asked, 'When was that?' 'O, a long time ago.' He knew no more, but being a good Ely man, added (with a sort of tongue in cheek look), 'That's where there wor a mad dog in the market and it bit a cart, so they tied that old cart up so it couldn't do no harm. And they do say that's where they goes fishing when they sees the moon in the water, try to stop un drowning.' Isn't it odd how so often humans see

---

[*] In total about £8,000, some £1,500,000 in today's money.

another community as comic? Irish jokes in the England of my youth; Polish jokes in New York; Belgian jokes in France. Even in the villages: to be coming from Burwell, a mile from so from Reach, would explain anything daft or stupid someone did.

But those riots... War – that long war against France that turned Europe upside down between 1793 and 1815 – was bad enough, and when a war ends the bills come in and there is always the problem of soldiers who no longer are wanted as soldiers and there are no jobs even for the able-bodied.[32] But there was also a run of years of terrible weather at that time, when harvests failed, and crops rotted in the fields. 1816 was especially bad – they called it 'The Year without a Summer' – and hunger and starvation stalked Europe. Work in the fields was impossible; men had nothing to feed their families. And the tax on imported grain was increased to help pay for the war.*

On top of all that, the new machines were making working hours harder in the big new industrial town, and they were destroying the income from piece work, mostly in spinning thread and weaving cloth, often done in cottages and little towns around the country. Unrest grew: the Luddite movement raided the factories to smash the cost-saving new machinery, which (they said) produced inferior goods and replaced skilled labour and drove down wages. Naturally, the Luddites were demonised in most of the press, and some mill owners took to shooting protesters. Eventually the Luddite movement was suppressed with full legal and military

* The terrible weather was caused by a series of volcanic eruptions in the Far East.

force, including hanging or transportation to Australia for those convicted.

The unrest of the cloth towns was reflected in the hungry countryside. In the Fenland, as elsewhere, so many had seen their age-old rights of common taken away by Enclosure and new ways of farming. With the price of bread going through the roof and farmers laying off workers because of the weather, hunger and unrest were rife. A serious riot broke out in Littleport, a few miles from Ely. Several men, who had met at the Globe Inn and tanked up on beer, began demanding money from and destroying the property of wealthier people. Rev. John Vachell, the vicar of St George's and one of the magistrates, read the 1714 Riot Act but nobody took any notice. The unrest spread to Ely. There, the magistrates tried to calm things down by ordering poor relief and fixing a minimum wage, but the next day, encouraged by a despatch from Lord Liverpool's government, an armed posse of the respectable citizens of Ely, backed by a detachment of the 1st Royal Dragoons which was stationed in Ely – their barracks were near where a pretty row of cottages now makes Parade Lane – went to Littleport, and attacked the rioters who had retreated to the George and Dragon. A soldier was injured, one rioter was killed, and at least one other went on the run.

The Bishop, Bowyer Sparke, as Prince of the Isle, had appointed Edward Christian (brother of Fletcher) as his Chief Justice in 1800. Christian was fully entitled to try the rioters alone. But Lord Liverpool's government appointed an emergency Special Commission, which had them tried in the imminent Assizes at Ely. Twenty three men and one woman were found guilty. Five were hanged.

On 28th June 1816, at 9am, William Beamiss, George Crow, John Dennis, Isaac Harley and Thomas South, were driven from the Bishop's Gaol, where they had been held – it is now Ely Museum – in a black-draped cart drawn by two horses. The bailiff's accounts say that cost five guineas, with thirteen shillings for the accompanying chaise for the Bishop's Gaol chaplain, John Griffin. (Someone has to keep accounts...)[33] Nobody in or around Ely was prepared to sell the rope required for the hanging, nor hire out a horse, cart or boy to lead the procession. When he submitted his expenses on 29th June, the High Bailiff, Francis Bagge noted, 'We have no power of pressing a cart for the purpose, and 'tis a difficult matter to get one, people feel's so much upon the occasion.' In the end, the authorities had to go to Cambridge to get a cart and a rope.

The procession was slow over the three quarters of a mile to Parnell Pits, in St. John's Road, where the gallows was – near the present Ely Scout Hut. They got there around 11am. The condemned were hanged after praying with the crowd for some time.

They played their part. They said what was always expected – almost a script – of condemned men. John Dennis said to the crowd,

All you who are witness in this, my disgraceful end, I exhort you, in the name of God, that God before whom I must shortly appear, to avoid drunkenness, Sabbath-breaking, whoremongery, and bad company: oh! beware of these sins. I pray you also to avoid rioting! and in every

respect refrain from breaking the laws of your country! – Remember the words of the Judge, that tried us for the crime, for which, we are now going to suffer, who said 'The law of the land will always be too strong for its assailants, and those who defy the law, will, in the end, be subdued by the law, and be compelled to submit to its justice or its mercy.' We stand here a melancholy example of the power and justice of the law. I freely forgive those who gave their evidence against me, and may the God of mercy forgive me, and have mercy on my soul!'

I wonder who wrote it for him?

The friends of the condemned men would have been asked to act as 'hangers on' for them as a final act of friendship – and mercy. By swinging on their legs, their deaths by strangulation would have been quicker. For death by hanging could be slow, and that makes one shiver on recalling the words of the formal sentence of death the judge could pronounce until 1969 – 'hanged by the neck <u>until</u> you are dead.' The long drop, which brought instant breaking of the neck and unconsciousness, was a generation in the Littleport men's future.

The coffined bodies were displayed for the rest of the day in a cottage in Gaol Street. Many people visited. They were buried the next day in St Mary's Church. A stone plaque was fixed to the south wall of the tower, which concluded, 'May their awful Fate be a warning to others'. It is still there.

John Griffin, the gaol chaplain, was unofficially given the ropes, which cost £1 5s 0d, after the hanging, which he kept. After he died the ropes passed to his housekeeper. She is said to have sold them as a cure for sore throats!

What a bitter coincidence! For Etheldreda was appealed to for help with throat complaints.

Those poor men would still just recognise the gaol, reborn as a delightful little museum. In places prisoners cut graffiti into the walls. I wonder what was the story of one Thomas Wilson, in prison for debt, carving his name, with some elegance and some knowledge of cursive script? What did '+ 21/77' mean? We shall never know.

The mid fourteenth century, pretty well anywhere in Europe, was not a good time to be around. Rapid, catastrophic climate change, which affected food supplies worldwide; the worst pandemic the world has seen in the last 2,000 years, which killed up to 55% of the people in a single winter; as a result, complete dislocation of 'normal' social structures, for with the price of labour going through the roof, nobody need stay tied to the land if they could get a job in a town which was crying out for labour. Laws passed after the Black Death to keep the price of labour down and the villeins in their hereditary place were ignored when they could safely be. As a result, there was a move to a money economy rather than one of customary services, in which people owed labour to the lord of their land: but nobody knew the rules for that new economy. There was widespread strife and the expensive scourge of war. Unrest everywhere, and resentment against the rich and the powerful, which boiled over more than once into murderous and indiscriminate civil violence. Merrie England, indeed.

The attempt by England's kings to make good their claim to the rich land of France was initially very successful. It was said at the time there was no woman so poor in England that she had not got a piece of jewellery won in France. It was, to start with, popular. But it dragged England into a costly war that lasted, with a few short breathers, for the best part of 100 years. By the 1370s the tide was turning against the English. As always, some people did very well out of war; most did not. As the Crown's need for money grew, taxation became more and more burdensome, and as always that fell upon the poor most of all. Richard II's government, led by the Archbishop of Canterbury, Simon of Sudbury, as Lord Chancellor, in early 1381 imposed a Poll Tax, which further increased that burden.

That seems to have been the last straw. All over the south east of England, people could stand no more, and began to gather in smaller, then larger, angry bands. The main body of what we now have to call rebels massed at Blackheath preparatory to a march on London. A priest from Kent, John Ball, already in trouble with the Church authorities over his loudly expressed heretical opinions, preached a series of inflammatory sermons in many towns. It is to his sermon before the group at Blackheath that is attributed one of the watchwords of the 'Peasants' Revolt' that followed:

> *'When Adam dalf, and Eve span, who was thanne a gentilman? From the beginning all men of kynde [nature] were created alike, and our bondage or servitude came in by the unjust oppression of naughty men…'*

Radical social thinking indeed, and not limited to England. In northern France, devastated by the wars of the great, that sentiment led to a class war, the Jacquerie, when the houses of the nobles and gentry were burned and their families slaughtered. It was far worse than anything seen in England, but what happened here was bad enough. On June 13, 1381, the mob, led by Wat Tyler, entered London in a sort of triumph: the gate of London Bridge was opened to them. They turned on innocent foreigners – one of the ugliest strands in mass unrest is nearly always xenophobia – and slaughtered the many peaceable Flemings, mainly in the cloth trade, who had lived in London for years. Geoffrey Chaucer – who lived through it all – mentions how 'Jakke Straw* and his meynee [band]' hunted them down. They rampaged down Fleet Street and into the Strand, burnt John of Gaunt's grand palace, the Savoy on the Strand, and seized – without any resistance by the guards – the Lord Chancellor from the Tower where he had taken refuge.

They dragged him to Tower Hill, and beheaded him with five (clumsy) sword blows. Young King Richard, with remarkable courage, confronted the now euphoric mob at Smithfield, outside the City. In a breach of all normal protocol, one of the leaders, Wat Tyler, spoke directly to him, with little sign of deference: and suddenly Lord Mayor Walworth stepped forward and stabbed him – the dagger is still on display in Fishmonger's Hall by the Thames. Richard's youth may have helped him, for he was only 14, and he shouted, 'I shall be your leader!', and promised reform. He may well have meant it: but he was not of age and his Council, dominated by his dreadful uncles, did not keep his

* Biography uncertain. he seems to have led the men from Essex.

promises. The rebellion was put down, and the leaders were all hanged.

Like many towns in East Anglia, Ely also had its own unrest. Two days after the rebels entered London, on a Saturday, news of their success came when the town was full of people come to market from the villages roundabout. Three Ely men, Richard de Leycester of 'Bocheristowe' (now Butchers' Row), Robert Buk, a fishmonger, and Adam Clymme, whipped up the crowd to fury with their speeches. Clymme told the peasantry to refuse all their customary labour services, as required by the manorial system, and to behead the lawyers – just like Jack Cade says in Shakespeare's *Henry VI*. Leycester called for the death of 'traitors to the king and the common people.'

These speeches were sparks to already combustible material. The crowd, now a mob, picked on three men, and lynched one, a prominent Ely lawyer, in the street. Next day Richard commandeered the Cathedral pulpit to urge the crowd to rise up 'on behalf of the king'. The day after that, a crowd attacked the Bishop's Gaol, which may well have been the gatehouse of the monastery that the present Porta replaced – that strong and forbidding statement of power and authority was only begun in 1397, perhaps even as a reaction to the recent unrest. Like the London mob, the Ely men also destroyed any court rolls and documents they could find, which among other things detailed those manorial obligations many of them so resented. Meanwhile, Leycester and Buk captured a local justice of the peace, Sir Edmund Walsyngham, killed him and stuck his head on the town pillory. But the crisis fizzled out quite soon, for there was no long term strategy to sustain real rebellion, or, as we might now say, regime change: the leaders were all hanged, or worse: John Ball was executed at St Albans while the young king watched (was he made to?): hanged by the neck, then disembowelled while still just alive, then his head was stuck on London Bridge and quarters of his body sent for display in four other towns. For a rebel's body must be destroyed as he had attempted to destroy the Body Politic.

'Peasants' Revolt', as we call it? Hardly. The leaders, wherever rioting took place, were not peasants: they were often men of some property and standing. In Ely, Richard de Leycester was a propertied man with two shops in Butchers' Row and goods totalling 40 marks (£26, which in today's money is some £20,000), Buk had land at Castlepath – now Castlehythe – and four shops and property in what is now Silver Street, and Clymme was worth £10 19s 5d, which is well over £8,000 in today's money. These three were not indigent: they obviously had some power and standing amongst the people of Ely, which is why the crowds listened to them.

It is hard to recall all this, when on a summer morning you walk up the hill with the dog and look at the cattle peacefully grazing with the Cathedral as photogenic backdrop, when at the quiet Green, you hear the noises of the town beginning to go about its daily business. It is only very rarely these days that you stub your mental toes on some of the hatred of the power and (once upon a time) wealth of the Church ingrained in some minds. I remember it in my youth as much more strong, perhaps because the CofE was so closely identified round here with the landed interest. For the alliance of power and wealth between Church and gentry *was* hated by many in these parts. I remember, when I first came down from the North, one old lady in the village saying to me that if old Squire Allix did not see you in Church on a Sunday you had no job on the Monday. An old man of the same fine vintage told me that as a boy the ticar's wife had struck him across the face with a riding crop for not touching his cap to her. Sanctity and selfless service – which can be documented – there was aplenty among the clergy, but what so many folk remembered and resented over the centuries was the burden of tithes and taxes, and the power to oppress and extort. Too often forgotten, as people remembered the pomp and showy majesty, was the provision through taxes and tithes and authority of hospitals, school, alms at the monastery door for the poor, building bridges, maintaining roads, providing work. Mediaeval monasteries were major economic and industrial engines, after all. But employers and taxmen and those richer than us are hardly ever popular, and were we in their shoes we could obviously always do things far better, could we not?

When you still were able to talk to real people in the Inland Revenue, I became quite friendly with my own tax inspector. He was a nice man, who loved his garden, and loved his job. He was a thoughtful fellow, who tried to persuade his clients that tax benefited everyone. (They might intellectually know that, but feeling it is something different.) At one of our meetings, he remarked, 'You know, I sometimes think that a good citizen should pay his taxes with the same delight as that with which a lover takes roses to his beloved.'

Dream on...

But power and wealth *can* be well used: the Ancients discussed and taught the Proper Use of Riches very often, and we would do well to build that once more into what we teach the young. There are reminders all around us not just of the power to punish and persecute but also of charity and compassion. In this town, spared so much of the 1960s horrors that ruined the centre of Cambridge and so many other towns, if you keep your eyes open, you keep stubbing your toes on a human past of charity as well as of suffering. Sometimes the dog takes us past what was St John's Farm, and along the busy road there is a sad, ancient wall, patched, overgrown and tumbledown. Its stone is a jumble: some cut Barnack, but also decaying Ely sandstone, that warm brown iron-rich stone so soft it will sometimes crumble to the touch. It was the boundary of what was the leper colony, on the edge of the town, looking out west. Long, long after the leper hospital closed, long after the road outside it had grown houses, a philanthropic couple founded and built, in 1917, an isolation hospital for diseases like scarlet fever: the first modern hospital Ely had.

The Leper Hospital of St. Mary Magdalene was founded to meet the same 12th century need to care for the many lepers as the Hospital of St. Mary Magdalene in Barnwell, by the railway at Cambridge's Stourbridge Common. About 1225 the Bishop of Ely gave the new hospital the church of Littleport, with its income from tithes. But quite soon after, Bishop Hugh of Northwold thought St. Mary Magdalene was endowed beyond its needs. (Possibly the urgency that drove its founding had passed with a retreat of the leprosy.) He amalgamated it with the older hospital of St. John Baptist, which the Cathedral Priory had founded: the new foundation was to consist of thirteen chaplains and brethren.

It's so easy to say 'leper hospital' and pass on. But unpack the words to find the horrible human reality. 'Mesel', people called them (from Latin *misellus*, 'pitiable'), or 'lazars', after Lazarus, who, his sufferings on this earth over, was in Abraham's bosom while Dives was in the pains of Hell. Attitudes were complex: were lepers enduring their Purgatory on earth, and therefore somehow sacred? Christ healed lepers – but only one of the ten, and he one of the despised Samaritans, came back to give thanks. But they must be cast out – isolated – for fear of infection. The hospitals could offer no cure, only palliative care as the disease took its slow and horrible course: no need to go into details. But they did offer a refuge. Endowed specifically to look after them to death, hospitals were often self-governing on the model of colleges, and sometimes the lepers might be better fed and housed than their healthy contemporaries.[34] Getting a place in a leper hospital was coveted, and 'leprous brothers and sisters' were accepted fully into the religious order of the house. But death was the only cure.

The hospitals were usually on the edge of towns – Cambridge probably had three, but only the plain Romanesque Chapel of the Barnwell Hospital survives. That would hold about 40 people, and that gives some idea of how common was the affliction. (Cambridge had some 3,000 people in the mid fourteenth century, at the very top of the curve of population growth before the devastating pandemic of the Black Death. The Poll Tax returns for Ely for 1377 show only 1,722 taxpayers, 1,902 for Cambridge.)[35] In the countryside the hospitals, 'lazar houses,' were often near crossroads or on the big highways, for lepers needed to be able to beg for alms, even trade in a small way, and in return would offer prayers for the souls of those who gave to them. The Barnwell hospital was placed to take advantage of the crowds who came to Cambridge's Stourbridge Fair and of the regular traffic along the high road to Norwich and Bury. Ely's hospitals of St John and St Mary were in the parish of St Mary, well outside the Cathedral precincts. They were near the Roman road, Akeman Street, which ran roughly on the line of the modern A10 from Durolipons – Cambridge. It probably went on across the Isle to Littleport, which would then have been, if not on the sea itself, on a tidal arm of the river. (It is unlikely it continued to Denver and then to the coast, as there was no high ground or roddon it could use across the marsh.)

To be diagnosed with leprosy – some tried to hide their symptoms – was awful. You were a source of fear, cast out for fear of the infection. You might go to a community, but effectively you were dead to society. (We know now the disease is less infectious than was then thought.) In common law there was provision, though it was not used a lot, and then only with caution, to remove lepers from society. A writ *de leproso amovendo* could force individuals out. One example from 1420: the Sheriff of Lincolnshire is told off for failing to have carried out an assessment of one John Louth, a Boston mercer, who (so it was said),

> *commonly mingles with the men of the aforesaid town and communicates with them in public as well as private places and refuses to remove himself to a place of solitude, as is customary and as it behoves him to do, to the serious danger of the aforesaid men and their manifest peril on account of the contagious nature of the aforesaid disease.*

We walk often past the graceful arches of what was the nave of the Ely hospital's chapel. They were infilled when the building, bereft of its chancel, was turned into a farmhouse, which it long remained. Other bits – a barn, a dovecot[36] – survive, because they were useful, but our forebears cleared much away: after all, they did not think about the past as we do.

I wonder, sometimes, whether the people who lived in that farmhouse for four centuries ever heard, in the stillness of the night, the ghosts of the prayers chanted in the chapel, and the suffering of the folk who chanted them. But they would be tired from the gruelling physical work of the farm, and probably slept the sleep of the just. Or thought it was the wind in the trees.

Behind and slightly to the north of the Lady Chapel, the Cathedral Chapter has had a physic garden planted against a south facing wall. On a warm summer day it is a place of delight to eye and nose. Labels unemphatically inform those who read them of the usefulness of these plants; their beauty is obvious. St John's wort for depression... valerian, a useful sedative... comfrey for sprains and broken bones... fennel, sometimes used as to suppress appetite, and good for nursing mothers and babies with colic... yarrow for headaches... sage as part of a toothpaste (yes, the ancestors did clean their teeth!), to soothe stings and to reduce fevers... lavender against fleas and moths – which is why washerwomen, who used it, were called laundresses. Rosemary was used for liver and gallbladder issues and poor appetite, and the indispensable garlic Greek and Roman physicians had recommended for infections, wounds, cancer, leprosy, heart problems, colds, and epilepsy and much else. (It may not work against some of the big hitters, but at least food tastes better.) Mugwort treated feet and women's problems, rue venomous bites, hyssop helped with coughs, wheezing and shortness of breath, and thyme is still used as an anti-fungal and anti-bacterial agent.

But to those who knew (and every monastery or convent however small would have a brother or a sister learned in the properties of herbs and how to use them) a well-stocked physic garden would be a pretty effective pharmacopeia. Of course the ancient Galenic theory of disease based on the four humours of Melancholy, Choler, Blood and Phlegm was wrong – though it has marked our language – but that does not preclude a pragmatic, and probably very ancient, awareness of the way diseases and complaints can be treated. After all, Merlin Sheldrake in his book *Entangled Life* relates how in an excavation in Spain just one of several Neanderthal individuals had tooth enamel with traces of use of an infection-killing fungus – and s/he had a tooth abscess. Distill the essence of the plant and preserve it – perhaps in alcohol – and you have the indisputable beginning of the rational curiosity that led to modern chemistry.[37]

It is well to remind out cynical selves that that knowledge and expertise would be shared even to the poorest in society if they asked for it. The rich had the poor on their conscience: in 1497 Thomas Parsons established a charity, still functioning, to house the indigent and aged. The religious houses had an explicit duty to feed the hungry and heal the sick – two of the Seven Works of Mercy enjoined by Christ himself. They did: the poor at the gate each day got their dole of food, the sick could draw on the wisdom and learning of the skilled herbalists.

Two of the modern great London teaching hospitals, St Thomas' and St Bartholomew's, began as religious houses. The new Physic Garden at Ely gracefully recalls the (certainly much bigger) one which the monastery had, which was lost at the Reformation. It is well to be reminded of the now too often ignored riches of plants, and of the charity of those who know their ways and use them. Where would we be without aspirin? Let us bless the unknown names of those who first decocted the leaves of willow to make that analgesic.

This is a place of healing. It is good to be here, to let the fever of the busy world outside be hushed for a spell, and watch the bees fumbling the flowers in their imperative way. The air is full of scent, and

> *above the milder sun*
> *Does through a fragrant zodiac run;*
> *And as it works, th' industrious bee*
> *Computes its time as well as we.*

As the sundial round the corner says, ΚΑΙΡΟΝ ΓΝΩΘΙ – 'Know when the time is right'.

Frost at Midnight

Remembrance Day. We came back to Reach from a fine rendering in my College Chapel of Victoria's great Mass, *Officium defunctorum,* of 1605, which he wrote for the Requiem of the Dowager Empress Maria, sister of Philip II of Spain. I was hungry, for when we had left home for the evening it was too early to eat. I was thinking of sardines on toast. There was the rime of the first frost of the winter on the car as we got back to it, and a clear sky. We drove back in silence, for there are some things to say that need no words. But as Rosanna stopped the car, switched off the lights, and we got out into the silent, starlit dark, 'Look!': for there above us was the magic of the Aurora Borealis, rarely seen so far south, which we had last seen together in the deep Arctic midwinter dark on the border between Norway and

Finland – when we had just found each other. Wave after wave of dreamily shifting light radiated, like diaphanous scarves, from the horizon, moving as gently and waving as delicately as fronds of weed in the slow sarabande of a smooth stream. So what, that we can explain them as energized particles from our sun crashing into Earth's upper atmosphere at up to 45 million mph, and then deflected by the planet's magnetic field? To say what a thing is made of or how it happens does not tell us what it is, just as to say a star is a mass of flaming gas only tells us what it is made of.

The scarves of energy are beautiful, awe-ful, utterly other, a dance in which man and his cleverness have no part except to offer wonder. The Sami of the northlands saw – see – the Lights as the spirits of the dead watching over the living and the world they loved – how fitting that we should see them that night! Sometimes, they say in the north, when the Aurora plays, the dogs hear the angels sing, but men's ears are stopped with things of earth. And I do in part believe it. And not just the aurora. For once, high in the mountains at the year's deep midnight, on the Swedish border, I was skiing alone on a still, moonless night of intense frost. The noise of skis and the creak of my poles in the snow seemed deafening. As I came out of the forest onto the frozen lake I stopped for breath: and I could almost swear I *heard* the dazzling stars crackling in that deep silence. [38]

We went out and stood on the bridge and tried to blank out the loom of the light of two villages and the towns around – more difficult than it used to be. We stood silent with our own thoughts. It was utterly quiet, still, not a breath stirring. A silent owl flew past on fimbriate wings: a good hunting night. A tiny 'snap' as a worn-out sycamore leaf broke free of its parent tree. With our new hearing aids we could hear it when it fell on the frosted ground. But then the dog nudged us, and I thought about sardines on toast, and we went in, grateful.

Our first winter with the House in Cow Lane. So much to do, so much to learn…

There came a great, and, as the world warms, an increasingly rare frost that lasted. And the surprise, for this droughty area, of a little snow. 'Will this last till Christmas?', people say instead of 'grand/dreadful/ funny weather' when you meet them in the street. 'Not had a white Christmas for years'. But the people on the stalls in the market, the lady selling *The Big Issue* in the High Street, are all bundled up like the Michelin man in the old advert, and I bet they don't want it to: it hit -10 degrees last night and we were cold in bed as we used regularly to be when I was young in an unheated house. This is weather when fingerless gloves are essential if you are serving on a market stall. But nobody could deny the unexpected, uncovenanted, *beauty* of this cold snap.

First frost, then a fog that coated everything with deep rime, that lasted all day and over the next night, and the next, catching and splintering the sunlight into dazzling shafts of brightness that try old eyes with a blinding glory. Spiders' webs glisten whitely in unsuspected places. The trees in the park by the Cathedral have finally dropped their last leaves all at once in fringes round them like lazily discarded clothes, and their bark has a shimmer from the soft patina of frost. With your finger you can write your ephemeral name on them.

The dog likes this weather, bounding as he is with energy, and this is the first time he has seen snow, even if it is not much more than a dusting. He licks it, he tries to eat it, he sneezes, he skids on it as I throw the dummy for him. Ah, youth, his springtime... he does not creak as I do now, watching my feet more than I used to, and glad of, if not using, the reassurance of my stick. We walk companionably down to the river, and for the first time for many years I see that the marina excavated from where once was Babylon has ice on it, and the river itself has floes drifting on the current, and the little backwaters have a web of cat ice. On the grass of the meadow the light snow lies even, untrodden, and it has been cold enough overnight for it to grow those magical ice flowers, with their infinite intricacy, and their complexity from simplicity of their fractal structure. I have not seen these since my *langlauf* skis crunched over them one winter when I was skiing alone high in a beloved valley in the Tyrol.

The thaw came, indeed, before Christmas. The blocking high over Scandinavia slipped sideways, and warm Atlantic air rushed in. The mercury rose 12 degrees in half that number of hours. Rain came with it. The frozen ground acquired a new and short-lived glory – damnable if you were driving or walking – of shining ice. Then even that melted. The frost had gone deep, and below the deep, deep puddles in the huge potholes the tractors had made on the droveways, the ground had swelled, and uncompacted, and the water that normally would have stayed splashily till spring then drained away through the newly opened interstices between stones and clay. I had never seen that happen before, or dry potholes in December. Oddly – yet I have known this many times before – it feels colder in the moist air than it did in the dry cold, and I am glad of the fire when we get home. Suddenly, I remember that in the house – a hovel, perhaps – that was on this site, up to the Reformation the householder would have had to pay to the Abbey the 'Ely farthing', a hearth tax levied on all households in every parish in the diocese. A farthing would then have bought a loaf of bread. I grew up when farthings were legal tender, and might be part of an advertised price, and somewhere I have a few of the tiny coins with, appropriately, the wren on the reverse of King George's head.

The wren busy getting its food in the cotoneaster outside the door shouts his remarkably loud call. Time for tea and buns as the December light fades. Nearly the shortest day: and as the rain stops, from the brightness under the clouds to the west there is a rumour of the returning sun.

Taking Root

I once heard a lecture by the writer Madeline Bunting, which began with questions we often glibly ask others, but rarely think deeply about for ourselves. 'Where do you feel you belong?' (It ought to have a follow-up: 'Or don't?') Some folk seem never to feel rooted anywhere and gad about, and are perfectly happy with that – so it seems. (But who knows what goes on inside?) Others, like me, make it tediously obvious that place matters. Land matters, where the copious summer sweat of your brow has made dark drips on dry soil, where the clinging mud of winter got under your nails and in the lines of your hardened hands. 'This plot', blessed or not, matters, as it mattered to others before you and matters now and (we hope) will matter to those who come after to tend what you tended. Perhaps it is, as the young might say, 'a countryman thing.' But I am not so sure, for I have known town friends for whom the street in Didsbury where they grew up, or the 1960s planned Cambridgeshire village where they were one of the pioneer residents, matters in the same sort of way: this is where I fit.

The sense of place can have extraordinary power. Some say wisdom sits in the place where you belong and are rooted. In Gaelic culture – what shreds of it are left after the terrible upheaval it has suffered in the last four centuries – people belong to the land, not the other way round. As W. G. Hoskins said, any 'place' is really a mix of physical location and people and time. Like this little city... The place will talk to you if you will simply pay attention, and listen. Don't be in a hurry. Memory is insistent, and slow, and attention is the key. I once had an idea of writing a biography (so to speak) of a single plot of land starting with the melting of the glaciers. It was one of those things that never got done, as the busy years hurried past. It was a good idea.

Making a garden has, of course, impressive Divine precedent. So we made one at Reach, Jenny and I, and Rosanna and I have made a very different one at Ely. The first has seen many changes, and quite a few mistakes, over the years, and it is a palimpsest of memory – of children playing (and quarrelling), and dogs, and the series of affable cats, and ducks, and geese and bees... and of times of great sadness and loss and even anger. It was not always summer: the winter wind blows keen.

I leave its trees, now mature, in trust to those who will come after me, and who will add their own stories to the palimpsest. The second garden was a *tabula rasa*; but its story has started well. But plans for what will grow and what will not, what will prosper and what will wither on the bough, are never certain.

For example… They warned us that global warming would bring new species to Britain: that was obvious, for 'nature' (from fungi to wildlife) is nothing if not opportunist. You never used to see hornets round here – something may not have suited them. But now I see odd ones quite often in summer. There are several hitherto unseen Continental varieties of wasp which I now see regularly; and while I am delightedly getting used to the way bits of the Fen have become so much richer in insects and birds since the National Trust (and some other smaller groups) began rewilding projects on their land, some newcomers are still glamorous enough to startle. But perhaps glamour is not everything.

This last September, we were sitting under the garden umbrella in the cooling evening with the dog asleep at our feet. Suddenly I noticed, on the underside of the umbrella's fabric, a really beautiful moth completely unknown to me. White, elegantly shaped, and with dark leading edges to its wings, it was about 3cm across. Now as a rather tiresome boy I prided myself on my knowledge of Butterflies and Moths of the British Isles – Richard South's book was a school prize which I knew almost by heart, and tried to tell others about it. (Youthful crazes do, sometimes, have useful effects long term.) But this moth was new, and I was about to go and search among that section of my library for help. But Rosanna beat me to it with her phone: yes, a newcomer, from Asia, which liked box bushes: a box moth. 'Hang on,' she said. 'That might explain why the box hedge has been looking poorly.' (I had put its tawny, desert brown patches down to my having cut that tricky plant at the wrong time.) Sure enough, when we looked the hedge was alive with caterpillars, and it is pretty certain the hedge will not recover: the twigs are already brittle.

If our hedge, why stop there? Is this going to be another of those things, like Dutch Elm disease, which will completely alter the face of the countryside? Box Hill, for ever linked in my mind with that crucial visit there in Jane Austen's *Emma*, without box trees? Old houses without knot gardens edged in box? That beautiful golden wood, best of all for the gentle art of wood engraving and once much used for making pipes and flutes, to grow more and more rare?

If the moth eats up all the box, will it survive? The elm beetle which carries the disease manages to keep going, moving in on any elm sucker that reaches more than a few inches in diameter. I suppose you would say it is in balance with its food plant... but here is one more unneeded reminder that nothing, nothing, stays as we always thought it would.

Gardens are important. But they are private pleasures. One of the best ways of beginning to feel grounded, in every sense, in a new place is to take on the discipline of an allotment. It is quite different to mere cultivation of your own garden, for it is inevitably very public and, for

241

someone like me, can't not be competitive. You cannot hide; the work of your hands is in the open. You soon get to know some of your fellow members of the Association, for they are very ready with advice, as you soon become yourself – if only in self-defence. Conversation will usually start with a grumble about the weather – too hot/dry/wet/cold (delete as appropriate) – or the condition of the soil, and quite soon can become advice (and you can give your own) of which the subtext might be, 'I wouldn't do it like that if I were you', 'That crop will never do well here', and so on. But it is a very relaxed, companionable way of making friends. We were wise to get an allotment almost as soon as we settled on getting the house.

This town is well provided with allotments – indeed, as I straightened up from lifting the main crop spuds I had grown there (Desiree, if you are interested), Philippa, who has a neighbouring plot to ours, told me that it was one of the few towns in England seeking to expand its provision of allotments. We have never had one in a town before, so how typical of the norm our experience is I don't know. Ours is on the slope of the ex-island on the solidest of glacial clays.[39] It's land that when wet sticks to everything, its tiny grains getting into the lines of your palm and your cuticles and stays stubbornly there, and it has to be scraped off spade or fork. When under a running tap you wash its clinginess off the carrots or spuds you have lifted, as the water drains away you have a little residue in the bottom of the sink of tiny grains, some glinting with mica: ground out of hard rocks by a long-forgotten glacier.

The land was like that, glue, when we first took it over, and I thought we'd never get it into a workable tilth.

It had been covered with black plastic sheeting so long that all that was to be turned up were the fleshy white, insidious, roots of convolvulus: and there were no worms, which is always a bad sign. Then that first summer we got the other extreme... dry and trodden, the soil was like concrete, and a fork however sharp had to be wiggled into it with your full weight on it. But it has its points: in this last spectacularly dry, hot summer, turn the earth as you lift the spuds – ready very early this year – and there is the slightest smell of damp, and the soil is darker with moisture retained between the grains. So the spuds – especially the Desirees, again – came up pretty decent, far better than I expected. I dug them alone, my back growling at me from bending to pick them up and put them into the bucket. I ached from the hard thrust of the fork into the stubborn earth and levering up the clods where I had trodden when there had been rain – I could just remember that rain, for it had been an appallingly dry and hot year.

And my mind flew back to the first allotment I had back in the village, and digging my main crop King Edwards with my father, to whom I was never very close, and him suddenly saying, 'Lad, as long as you are digging spuds my Dad will never be dead,' An astonishingly moving moment, of which neither of us knew how to speak, but a sudden glimpse into my father's childhood in Staffordshire, and – well, what? For he never spoke of his father. Digging up the past: memories, feelings, erupt like the fertile tubers from the broken soil which looks so hard to work. To catch up, so to speak, with your own life (and your culture's history) is not nostalgia or indulgence: it getting things in perspective, like tidying up a room. I wish my father had spoken of his past.

Where was I? Oh yes, telling you about the allotment. There is, as they say (but here it is true), a real sense of community among fellow allotment holders. (A visitor from Hereford to the allotments, whom I did not know, said to me as she walked past, 'You can tell you have a wonderful community here.') I don't know what it is like on the other sites: each community seems to keep aloof from the others – after all, the land we work is quite different, and therefore so are the problems. I sometimes drive past the allotments down on the peat fen, and have caught myself envying the ease of working that land, light to hoe and spade: but then, open to the searing blasts of winter wind and in a wet year sticky and in a dry one dust. (Envy is always shortsighted.) Our community: men who have grown up in the town, and known it all their lives; a couple of people who scribble for a sort of living, like me; an engineer; a retired farmer who likes to use the fearsome chemicals he used on his farm, which nobody else does; a man who opens the big gates with one hand while leaning on his walking frame; the owner of one of the better restaurants in the town, who loves to grow squashes organically for his dishes; a man who has been in England for forty years since he came from far away, and says this country has been good to him, but the language still trips him up; a young couple trying to be self-sufficient; people whose plots riot in colour, or whose artichokes are allowed to grow to their magnificent efflorescence – a reminder of a magic moment when, crossing the *puszta* in Hungary by train, I once saw a huge field of them flash past, all magnificently blooming to the desert air. And there are people whose onions grow to a bronzed and smooth rotundity mine on this land never manage. (They did on the land at Reach.) There are plots with carpets down between the rows to check the weeds, plots immaculate and regimented, standing to attention, plots in contrast where vegetable liberty reigns and there is no discrimination against weeds, and plots like ours, near the Community Shed where you can keep your tools and the community grasscutters for trimming the paths. Being there, I am always trying and never quite succeeding to make it not disgrace us under the many eyes that see it. Convolvulus is a sly, subtle, fast-moving enemy, trumpeting your failure in sudden glory of huge white blooms. Damned stuff: I don't know a single gardener who likes it.

John's plot is next to mine. He has had it for years, and it has been a picture of plenty. His strawberries were cosseted with straw and shielded by netting from attentive blackbirds (who love them). His onions rounded into fat gold globes, with never a sign of neck rot. His early spuds were the earliest on the plate. But that clay... and John's plot last year was only a reminder of its glory, for convolvulus gained a small victory and was left to gloat, the strawberries were not strawed, and the borders were not mown. I saw him in the town coming back from the market with vegetables in his basket. Sprightly and cheerful as ever, he caught my glance down. 'Yes, I am giving it up. It's been good, but it is good to know when to stop. I can't bend as I did.' Nor can I, John, nor can I.

One day I too will have to decide to walk back from town with bought vegetables. For the land remains, and must pass on to someone else who will cherish it and be able to use it well.

Not quite but nearly the hottest day of a hot year was scheduled for the yearly Allotment Barbecue: the first we had been to. The committee did not know the weather forecast at the time of planning... But *of course* we go ahead – in a temperature of 32 degrees. The tables groan – not a cliché for they *did* audibly creak on the little uneven lawn by the Shed – with food people have contributed. Hilary and her daughter have set out chairs and benches. Philippa, urbane and efficient by the barbecue, turns the sausages and lamb koftas and burgers. Conversation ranges: obviously, weather, rainfall, heat are opening gambits with those one has not met before. But Philippa and I get onto General Crises in history, the current instability in the North Atlantic Drift, her time working in Labrador. Ali and his wife are into local archaeology – not that any of us have found much on our plots, not even bits of clay pipe. Someone has brought a cold roast chicken, beautifully and evenly browned, spatchcocked and laid out, limbs aspread in the French manner, so that it looks exactly like a huge toad – and we do have some resident toads, thank Heaven. Two slices of hardboiled egg with a half olive on each complete the eyes. Next to it, and the plenitude of salads, a beautiful cherry cake, made in a mould with a sweet pastry crust. I have had worse in a good *patisserie* in France. It turns out that another neighbour, Annie, is an internationally known food writer and broadcaster, and we talk enthusiastically about food we have eaten, recipes we know for pigeon and muntjac, and the sweetness of mediaeval food and why Madeira has a sugar loaf on its coat of arms. Vegetable growing, like walking a dog, is a great builder of bridges, and the sharing of food together – well, it is one of the (shall I say?) sacred things that makes us human.

The afternoon has got hotter, and the sun beats pitilessly down on sunhats and umbrellas. 'His going forth is from the end of the heaven, and his circuit unto the ends of it: and there is nothing hid from the heat thereof.' No, indeed; but, replete and full of good humour and companionship, we feel we can pardon even that heat in the post-lunch languor of long afternoon.

And tomorrow, another day of heat, and after Mass, the Church barbecue in the ancient churchyard, where (unlike here) there is lots of archaeology beneath the quiet trees, among the companionable graves of our even-Christen. They would have known all about worry about the crops and the weather, and the summer's heat, and looked forward to harvest. For soon, in early September, the Allotments will be a clamour of sunflowers, squashes will laze across the ground where I dug the new potatoes. A precocious bramble in the hedge already reaches out and grabs me. They do it deliberately, I know, and they draw blood much more readily from my old skin than they used to – if slime moulds can solve problems, then why should not a bramble decide to be awkward? (Actually, their thorns serve double purpose: as the wind stirs their long droop, they can latch on to grass or ground, and take root: and the bramble thicket grows even bigger. And, as it happens, become a wonderful habitat for little creatures and a nurse for more distinguished trees.) But Philippa does grow wonderful blackberries, and Hilary sumptuous raspberries, far more than they can eat, and I shall have beetroot and three varieties of tomato to give away in exchange – I say with no little pride that the best beetroot I have grown on this land weighed 6lb, the size of the mangelwurzels out of which people made jam in the thin years when I was a child. I once grew a tomato that weighed 24 ounces. Nearby, at the house, the apples, diagonally trained along the wall we built round My Lady's garden, promise the juicy fulfilment of quiet autumn.

...A golden summer evening in that maturing walled garden. My Lady has planted lots of plants that scent the air, plants good for healing, plants that offer plenteous nectar to butterflies and the fumbling bees of all sizes. Friends are round, sharing a bottle of wine. Quiet, save for the occasional scream from the road through the town of a motorbike in too low a gear for the macho speed the lad (ah, youth!) feels he has to use to get from one traffic light to the next. It highlights the quiet.

The bees are busy in the clematis and honeysuckle. But... that isn't a bee! We have been honoured by a visit from a humming bird hawk moth, a delicate creature the size of the humming birds I have seen in the islands of the Caribbean, wings going too fast to see as it hovers and inserts its long proboscis into the calyx of its chosen bloom. Satisfied, it jerks away to another bloom. It brought, and took, sweetness to the garden, just as one did when I saw my first one, sitting with friends over post prandial wine in their garden as the westering sun lit up the distant snows on Mont Blanc far away across the lake.

And what a wonderful example of convergent evolution! A bird, with a heart and vascular system like any other bird, and an insect with spiracles, of a quite different phylum, have independently both evolved the physique and tools to take advantage of an ecological niche to the point where at a quick glance you could mistake one for the other. Just so the sabre-toothed tiger evolved in Eurasia, but also in the Americas, and they looked identical and had the same diet. But one was a placental and the other a marsupial mammal. What a wonderful world!

On the sandstone step which I put by the door, a patch of lichen catches the light. Lichens grow slowly, so slowly, on stone, eating it into (one day) soil. Transplanted trees can thrive. If you get the time right.

Time…

Diversions and Distractions

[1] See Essay 1 of *Essays on Picturesque Beauty; On Picturesque Travel;* and *On Sketching Landscape, London,* 1792): 'Ideas of beauty vary with the object, and with the eye of the spectator. Those artificial forms appear generally the most beautiful with which we have been the most Conversant.'

[2] W. Gilpin: *Observations on several parts of the Counties of Cambridge, Norfolk, Suffolk and Essex. Also on several parts of North Wales; relative chiefly to picturesque beauty. in two tours, the Former made in the year 1769, the latter in the year 1773.* (London, 1809 ed.). He deserved the fun poked at him by William Combe and Thomas Rowlandson in their illustrated *Tours of Dr Syntax* (1809-21). (Nowadays, alas, booksellers often break up the books to sell Rowlandson's prints separately – you make a better profit like that.)

[3] I have loved that simile of Milton's is Book 1 of *Paradise Lost* (lines 795 ff.) ever since I came across it first when my beard had yet to grow, and I used to quote it to my bees when a good honey flow was on:

As bees
In spring-time, when the Sun with Taurus rides.
Pour forth their populous youth about the hive
In clusters; they among fresh dews and flowers
Fly to and fro, or on the smoothed plank,
The suburb of their straw-built citadel,
New rubbed with balm, expatiate, and confer
Their state-affairs:

But he is deliberately using this glimpse of wholesome springtime to contrast with the devils in Hell. I would not wish to suggest people walking about the marketplace, stopping and talking, are devils.

[4] He shows the houses lining the streets, apparently backing on to gardens or even enclosed fields. It is so easy to forget that when your main motive power is horses, they need grazing and paddocks even in the middle of towns.

[5] An uncle of mine who was head foundryman at the Goldendale blast furnace in Tunstall, Staffordshire, got a daily allowance of 8 pints of weak beer because of the heat of the work. I was there once when they tapped the furnace and it was hot indeed. The molten iron ran in a torrent of flame into the sand moulds – laid out for all the world like a sow and her piglets. Hence pig iron.

[6] Though it is a matter of some surprise that according to Peter Spufford's research (*Power and Profit: the Merchant in Medieval Europe* (London, Thames and Hudson, 2002) one of the largest markets for fresh saltwater fish in the fourteenth century was Coventry!

[7] I have come across this nickname more than once, but am unsure as to how ancient and widespread it really is. Bagpipes were played all over England in various forms – Chaucer's Miller plays one as the pilgrims

leave Southwark – but the single-piped Lincolnshire version must have had a distinctive enough tone to give point to the banter between Falstaff and Hal in Shakespeare's *I Henry IV* I.ii: '*Falstaff:* 'Sblood, I am as melancholy as a gib cat or a lugged bear. *Hal:* Or an old lion, or a lover's lute. *Falstaff:* Yea, or the drone of a Lincolnshire bagpipe.' Do courting frogs (and/or toads) sound like that? I suppose so.

[8] At the age of 12 she was married to Æþelræd Unræde, Ethelred the Ill-Counselled, by whom she had Edward, later King and Confessor, who is claimed as founder by the King's School at Ely. Later, she married Canute, by whom she had Harthacanute, whom Sellars and Yeatman in *1066 and All That* call 'Halfacanute.'

[9] I have often puzzled about that number. When you think what Stuntney and Littleport just down the road were worth to the monastery, it seems a very small payment for a great deal of stone. I wonder whether it was simply a token, a sort of licence asserting a right of ownership but waiving the real market value? I would like to think so. And the value of that payment would certainly not have covered the costs of extraction and transport of the stone, which would have been many times the raw cost.

[10] Or so most people say, claiming the mediaeval precinct boundary ran along Stepil Lane/ High Street, Fore Hill down to the river, along the riverside (Broad Street/ Flax Lane), then up Back Lane and Fountain Lane, to what is now St Mary's Street. But there are problems, not without interest to oddballs like me. It's not impossible for a parish church like St Mary's to be inside a monastery precinct, for the lost St Cross was against the north wall of the cathedral, but it is not common. But if the boundary in the 14th century was as above, why did Prior Walpole build the great Porta where it is, well inside that circumference, and facing onto an old lane, the Gallarye[sic]? Why does Speed's 1610 map show a lane from the Porta down to Broad Street, neatly separating the earthworks of the bailey from Dean's Meadow, and what is a motte doing inside the monastic precincts? Was that motte built by William the Bastard, or as a defence by Hereward the Wake when he held Ely against him, or by Bishop Nigel during the Anarchy of the 1130s and 40s against King Stephen? Could it be its use was always more peaceable, and the Motte is the base of a mill tump, as shown on Speed's map? (I owe thanks to my friend Felix Jackson, Custodian of Ely Museum, discussion with whom prompted these questions. And there are more…)

[11] Similarly, another mediaeval name, 'The Angel and Salutation', recalling he Annunciation to the Blessed Virgin, became just 'The Angel', or, more rarely, 'the Salutation' (as in Ambleside and about 16 other English places). 'God encompasseth us' became 'Goat and Compasses.'

[12] For example, William Frederick ('Mad') Wyndham, (1840-66) the heir to Felbrigg Hall in Norfolk, of whom R. W. Ketton-Cremer writes in his delightful *Felbrigg: The Story of a House*, (London, Rupert Hart-Davis, 1962).

¹³ On the night of 12–13 February 1322, fortunately just after matins had finished at about 04.30, otherwise the monks would have been in their stalls. It might have been a result of digging foundations for the ambitious new Lady Chapel, which allowed water into the footings of the tower. It was not the only central tower to collapse: it happened at Winchester and Lincoln, and Salisbury's piers began to bulge – but catastrophe was avoided by the insertion of scissor arches.

¹⁴ His epitaph – he died in 1363 and was buried below the Octagon – described him as *flos operatorum*, 'the flower of craftsmen', and he was trained as a goldsmith. But it also recorded his purchases for the house of Brame and Mepal as well as building of the Octagon, and was clearly praising his administrative rather than architectural skills.

¹⁵ Why make difficulties for yourself by stretching the technology and the materials to the very limits? The length is not mere random choice – none is in the building – but part of the mystical mathematical coding of all great religious buildings... it gets absorbingly complicated: try for starters Robert Lawlor, *Sacred Geometry: Philosophy and Practice* (1982) and Robert Foster, *Patterns of Thought: Hidden Meaning of the Great Pavement of Westminster Abbey* (1991). Each mason's and carpenter's workshop had its own standard of measurement – weights and measures would not be more than approximate for some centuries yet – and the mediaeval foot varied slightly, often shorter than the modern. A common mason's measure was a foot of 11 and a half inches. If one comparable to that was used by the architect, the height becomes 63 'feet': 7 X 32. That number symbolises The Seven Days of Creation, the Seven Gifts of the Spirit, multiplied by the square of the Trinity, in a structure of eight sides, 8 signifying resurrection and rebirth.

¹⁶ Epigram 99: *Bascauda: Barbara de pictis veni bascauda Britannis,/sed me iam mavult dicere Roma suam.* 'A BASKET: I came from the painted Britons, but now Rome prefers to call me her own.'

¹⁷ In his *Libellus de consecratione ecclesiae S. Dionysii*, describing the work he did in rebuilding the Abbey of St Denis in Paris, the first great example of the Gothic style. Of course, he would also have said, 'To the glory of God'.

¹⁸ After the Dissolution, the loss of the Abbey community as employer, and of pilgrims coming to Etheldreda's shrine, the town rapidly declined. Only with the grand drainage schemes of the seventeenth and eighteenth centuries, and the arrival of the railway in 1845, did things improve. Up till then the town maps show the city had if anything shrunk from the limits shown in Speed's map of 1610. The decline in ecclesiastical management of the fen and waterways led to more flooding, and several visitors commented on how wet and muddy the town was: Celia Fiennes in the 1690s, and Daniel Defoe in the early 18th Century, noted, as well as the city's market gardens, its overflowing wells.

¹⁹ That is, it is not subject to the jurisdiction of the diocese or City that surrounds it, but to the Bishop, Prince of the Isle of Ely as Etheldreda's successor. Just so, the Chapels Royal and other royal peculiars are not subject to the jurisdiction of the Bishop of London in whose Diocese they stand, but directly to the Crown. The colleges of Cambridge are also peculiars, not subject to the authority of the Bishop of the diocese in which they stand.

²⁰ Tennyson's 'Northern Farmer, New Style', puts it well:
Do'ant be stunt; taäke time.
I knaws what maäkes tha sa mad.
Warn't I craäzed fur the lasses mysén when I wur a lad?
But I knaw'd a Quaäker feller as often 'as towd ma this:
'Doänt thou marry for munny, but goä wheer munny is!
An' I went wheer munny war; an' thy muther coom to 'and,
Wi' lots o' munny laaïd by, an' a nicetish bit o' land.
Maäybe she warn't a beauty—I niver giv it a thowt—
But warn't she as good to cuddle an' kiss as a lass as 'ant nowt?

²¹ It was originally the gateway to the burial ground of the parish church of the Holy Cross, of which no trace above ground now remains, which abutted on the north side of the nave of the Cathedral. Later the parishioners of Holy Trinity, when it was established in the Lady Chapel in 1566, used it. Steeple Gate also housed the parish bell.

²² Cutlack and Harlock's Quayside Brewery was taken over by the Norwich firm of Steward and Patterson, who once had 650 or so pubs. They were then taken over by Watney Mann in 1963, who closed the Ely brewery down in 1970.

²³ But the feasibility of a surprise landing from the north German islands had been blown by Erskine Childers' fine and very popular novel, *The Riddle of the Sands* (1903), which may indeed have led to a change in strategy on the part both of the War Office and of the German High Command.

²⁴ Other palatinates included Durham, Chester and Lancaster – which is why we Lancastrians still toast the Duke of Lancaster rather than the King after dinner – important counties on the marches against the Welsh and the Scots, where the prince ruled semi-autonomously. Only in 1830 were these palatinate jurisdictions abolished.

²⁵ Interesting facts you may not want to know: this stone was much valued in the 12th century, and was much to the taste of Henry of Blois, King Stephen's brother, Cardinal and Bishop of Winchester. Seven fonts are known in England, most in Hampshire, all weighing over 2 tons, sculpted from the same block, quarried near the river Escaut. Several tombstones also exist, of which this is perhaps the finest.

²⁶ I have always treasured that remark of another diplomat, Sir Henry Wootton, who on a mission to Augsburg in 1604 said, with delicious ambiguity, that an ambassador 'is an honest gentleman sent to lie abroad [our sense, or the contemporary sense of 'stay'] for the good of his country'.

²⁷ Interesting clue to what the Saxon church built by Aethelwold of Winchester after 970 might have looked like. Brixworth in Northamptonshire also had *portici*, before the Normans mucked it about. (No English Heritage to bother about then...)

²⁸ Some think the bailey dates from when Bishop Nigel fortified the Isle against King Stephen, sometime early in the civil war that engulfed his reign. (see p. 204)

²⁹ Towns with pigeons and high buildings are ideal territory for them. A friend of mine had for years an office high up on London's Millbank Tower: lucky man, each year peregrines nested on his windowsill.

³⁰ He was a parish or petty constable, was unpaid, and was responsible for organising the Watch (also unpaid) and for the enforcement of law, including the hue and cry which allowed victims of a crime to summon neighbours to pursue suspected criminals. The position – sometimes called headborough – evolved from the ancient office of 'chief pledge' of an administrative unit called a tithing, and was part of an ancient system whereby a community policed itself. It was easy to make fun of the office, as Shakespeare does in his Dogberry in *Much Ado about Nothing*, but until Henry Fielding, the novelist and magistrate, and his brother, set up the Bow Street runners in 1749, there was nothing else and on the whole the system worked in a small society where most people knew each other. Sorry about that long note... but I find this sort of thing interesting.

³¹ Probably one of his sermons, later collected in *Holsome and Catholyke Doctryne concerning the Seven Sacramentes of Chrystes Church, expedient to be knowen of all men, set forth in maner of Shorte Sermons to bee made to the People* (London, 1558). That Wolsey could read this with intelligence says a lot about the level of literacy in humble folk at the time.

³² Kipling knew all about it: His poem 'Tommy' starts
> I went into a public 'ouse to get a pint o' beer,
> The publican 'e up an' sez, 'We serve no red-coats here.'
> The girls be'ind the bar they laughed an' giggled fit to die,
> I outs into the street again an' to myself sez I:
> O it's Tommy this, an' Tommy that, an' 'Tommy, go away';
> But it's 'Thank you, Mister Atkins,' when the band begins to play
> The band begins to play, my boys, the band begins to play,
> O it's 'Thank you, Mister Atkins,' when the band begins to play.

³³ Yes indeed. In the Parker Library in Corpus Christi College, Cambridge is a handwritten note detailing what the figs and nuts for Archbishop Cranmer's last breakfast cost, and the price of the faggots (1d) for his burning that morning.

34   There is some evidence that when the disease became less common, or its diagnosis improved, there was spare capacity, as we say, and places in the often well-endowed hospitals were sought by perfectly healthy people. Indeed, by the 14th century, some foundations seem to have been struggling to fill their numbers with genuine lepers. There are complaints: at the Hospital of St Giles at Boughton, near Chester, for example, two married lepers, Robert and Agnes Waldshaf, petitioned the crown around 1328, complaining that the hospital founded 'for lepers alone…is now charged with other folk who are not sick', and asked 'that they might be served with what he [the King] granted them there'.

35   Every lay person over 14 who was not a beggar had to pay a groat (4d). It remained by our standards not much more than a large village: a survey of 1416 recorded 457 buildings, in a core established street pattern recognisable today; by 1563 there were 800 households.

36   Dovecots: a grand source of pigeon muck to put on the land – and by golly, they are incontinent and productive birds – and a source of the delicious young squabs, especially welcome in the hungry time, early spring, when as yet there was little to eat.

37   The mediaeval world's conviction that Creation was not a meaningless place but made discoverable sense in every corner, and that everything had a property that connected it in some way to everything else, is fundamental to the scientific outlook. The crass and ignorant slander so common even among people who should know better – let alone the deplorable media – that the mediaeval people were stupid and that things are so much better and we are so much cleverer now gets my goat. It is easily demonstrable as palpably false. We are the dwarves standing on their giant shoulders. But that is another book…

38   Laurens van der Post in *The Heart of the Hunter*, (London, Hogarth, 1961) suggested that the stars made a crackling sound that dogs could hear and to which they would respond. Similarly with the aurora: there are persistent reports from travellers in the far north of the aurora making its own strange music. The Saami people call the aurora 'guovssahas' – the light that can be heard, a lovely phrase – and there is a remarkable similarity in descriptions of these sounds across cultures from Siberia to Norway. Current science is no longer quite prepared to dismiss that sort of thing. In 2012 researchers from Aalto University in Finland recorded whipping or cracking sounds during an aurora, which they said seemed to be formed some 200 feet above ground level. How, they did not explain. But note the shift in assumptions revealed in what those researchers could say in 2014: 'details about how the auroral sounds are *created* (my italics) are still a mystery'.

39   To be exact, Ely sits atop an area of glacial deposits, making it one of the highest points in the surrounding countryside at 40 metres (133 feet) above sea level. That is some advantage with global warming. People forget that the Cam, which flows into the Ouse, is naturally tidal already nearly as far as Cambridge.